Finishing Touches

The Art of Cake Decorating

Finishing Touches

Pat Ashby and Tombi Peck

Photography by Melvin Grey

MEREHURST PRESS
LONDON

Published 1986 by Merehurst Press
Ferry House, 51/57 Lacy Road,
Putney, London SW15 1PR
Reprinted with amendments 1986
Reprinted 1987
Reprinted 1988
Reprinted 1989

ISBN 0 948075 03 1 (cased)
ISBN 1 85391 093 7 (limp)

Edited by Joyce Becker, assisted by Suzanne Ellis
Designed by Roger Daniels
Photographed by Melvin Grey, assisted by Trudi Ballantyne
Typeset by Lineage
Colour separation by Fotographics Ltd, London-Hong Kong
Printed in Belgium by Proost International Book Production

ACKNOWLEDGEMENTS

Pat Ashby would like to thank George Ashby,
Carolyn Duncan and Barbara Nayler for their
help in the preparation of this book.

Tombi Peck would like to thank Sally Collier,
David Colbourne, Janet Foster, Ivy Gray,
Norma Laver, Maggie and Rosie Peck, and
Pat Waller for their help in the preparation
of this book.

The publishers would like to thank the staff
of B. R. Mathews, 12 Gipsy Hill, London, SE19, UK
for their assistance, and for supplying the cake
decorating equipment for photography. Additional
equipment supplied by Orchard Products.

The publishers would like to thank Tate & Lyle Sugars for
their encouragement and support.

Contents

Introduction

Cake Decorating Equipment

Good equipment is essential for the cake decorator. High quality tools can be purchased from specialist shops or large department stores, while other useful items can be found in the kitchen, sewing box or tool box. The cake decorating equipment shown here is just a selection of items which most decorators use.

Turntable – A good turntable is essential. Choose one which is fairly heavy, with smooth turning. A tilting feature with a separate angled bearing is useful. Clips are needed for use in the tilted position, or for holding a light dummy.

Work surface – There are several different special plastic or nylon boards on the market.

Rolling pin – An ordinary wooden rolling pin is necessary for rolling out marzipan and sugarpaste. For rolling out modelling or flower paste, use a small rolling pin made from special plastic or finely sanded wood.

Piping tubes – There are several different types on the market. Nickel-plated ones are often more accurately made, which is very important for fine piping with the smaller gauges. Brass tubes have a wider base and need a wider bag.

Cocktail sticks – Use good quality wooden ones.

Ball tools – These come in many different types. Most decorators use smooth plastic ones.

Scissors – A selection of different scissors is necessary. Fine-bladed nail scissors, both with straight and curved points, embroidery scissors and large craft or floristry scissors are all useful.

Knives – Choose good quality, sharp-bladed kitchen knives, craft knives and modelling knives.

Crimpers – Choose a selection of different crimpers for working on sugarpaste.

Moulds – There is a variety of moulds available for chocolate work, pastillage, etc.

Palette knives – An ordinary kitchen palette knife and a crank-handled artist's palette knife are both useful.

Drying racks – Various plastic, metal and wooden forms are useful for drying cut-out shapes.

Wooden skewers, dowelling and plastic knitting needles with heads removed – These have a variety of uses in cake decorating.

Edible colouring – This is available in paste, liquid and powder forms, and is used to colour icing and pastes.

Gum tragacanth – This is a fine powder which is an important ingredient in flower paste and some modelling pastes. Pastes made with gum tragacanth become very hard when dry.

Paint brushes – Artist's brushes in various sizes are used for brush embroidery, painting on details and brushing on petal dust.

Cake boards – Silver or gold cake boards are available in the same sizes and shapes as cake pans.

Papers – A cake decorator needs greaseproof paper, wax paper, roasting wrap and foils.

Icing smoothers – A plastic or metal scraper is necessary for royal icing. Plastic smoothers with handles are used for sugarpaste.

Metal straight edge – This is useful for smoothing icing and for positioning decorations.

Cutters – Plastic or metal cutters are used for cutting out marzipan, modelling paste and flower paste. The Garrett frill is a specially designed cutter for making sugarpaste frills.

Recipes for Cakes

Every beautifully decorated cake in this book needs a well-baked cake for its base. The four recipes given here have all been tested using metric, Imperial and American measurements. Use one set of measurements only.

Cake tins or pans should be about two-thirds filled with mixture before baking. Remember that round and square pans of the same dimensions will need different amounts of mixture. A good rule is that a square tin will hold the same amount as a round tin which is 2.5-3cm (1-1½in) larger in diameter: the same amount of mixture will fill a 15cm (6in) square tin or an 18cm (7in) round tin.

If making cakes in heart-shaped, octagonal or other shaped tins, measure how much water the tin will hold, then find the correct-sized round or square tin which will hold the same amount. Make enough cake mixture to fill the round or square tin. It may be necessary to vary baking times with irregular-shaped pans, so check during baking.

the fruit from coming through and overcooking. Smooth the surface. Wrap a double layer of brown paper around the outside of the tin.

Bake at 140°C (275°F/Gas Mark 1) for about 5-6 hours, or until top is brown and the sides begin to shrink away from the tin.

Leave until cold before storing.

Light Fruit Cake

Use this fruit cake for any of the celebration cakes in this book. The mixture will make a 18cm (7in) square cake, or equivalent.

150g (6oz/1 cup) raisins
150g (6oz/1 cup) sultanas (golden raisins)
150g (6oz/1 cup) currants
75g (3oz/¾ cup) glacé cherries, quartered
50g (2oz/½ cup) chopped mixed peel
125ml (4fl oz/½ cup) dry sherry
60ml (2 tablespoons) finely chopped almonds

Place the fruit, peel and almonds in a plastic bowl, pour over the sherry, cover and leave for at least 12 hours.

Very Rich Fruit Cake

This mixture will make a 30cm (12in) square cake or the equivalent. It is a rich, firm-textured cake and provides an excellent base for decorating.

1kg (2lb/8 cups) raisins
1kg (2lb/8 cups) sultanas (golden raisins)
500g (1lb/4 cups) currants
250g (8oz/2 cups) glacé cherries, halved
125g (4oz/1 cup) glacé apricots, chopped
125g (4oz/1 cup) glacé pineapple, chopped
200ml (5fl oz/½ cup) brandy

Wash and dry the fruit and place in a plastic bowl which has a tight-fitting lid. Pour the brandy over the fruit, seal the bowl and leave in a cool place to marinate for one week.

500g (1lb/2 cups) butter
500g (1lb/2 cups) soft dark brown sugar
20ml (4 teaspoons) apricot jam
20ml (4 teaspoons) golden syrup (corn syrup)
20ml (4 teaspoons) molasses
500g (1lb/4 cups) plain (all-purpose) flour
2.5ml (½ teaspoon) bicarbonate of soda (baking soda)

5ml (1 teaspoon) each ground allspice, cinnamon, cloves, ginger and nutmeg
2.5ml (½ teaspoon) ground mace
250g (8oz/1½ cups) ground almonds
10 large eggs
500g (1lb/2 cups) dates, very finely chopped
250g (8oz/1½ cups) blanched almonds, split

Cream the butter until soft. Gradually add the sugar and cream well. Stir in the jam, syrup and molasses.

Sift together the flour, spices and bicarbonate of soda. Stir in the ground almonds.

Add the eggs to the creamed mixture one at a time alternately with the sifted flour. Beat well after each addition. Do not add the eggs too quickly or the mixture may curdle.

Set aside about 250ml (8fl oz/ 1 cup) of the batter. Stir the dates and almonds into the remaining batter, then stir in the brandied fruit.

Prepare the cake tin by greasing with butter and lining with silicone or greaseproof paper. Spread half of the unfruited batter evenly on the bottom of the tin. Fill with the fruited batter and top with the remaining unfruited batter. The layers of unfruited batter prevent

150g (6oz/¾ cup) butter
150g (6oz/¾ cup) soft dark brown sugar
20ml (4 teaspoons) black treacle or molasses
3 medium-sized eggs
150g (6oz/1½ cups) plain (all-purpose) flour
25g (1oz/¼ cup) self-raising flour
2.5ml (½ teaspoon) ground mixed spice
2.5ml (½ teaspoon) ground cinnamon
1.5ml (¼ teaspoon) ground nutmeg
1.5ml (¼ teaspoon) salt

Cream the butter and sugar until fluffy, then beat in the treacle or molasses.

Beat the eggs together, then beat into the creamed mixture a little at a time.

Sift together the flours, spices and salt. Stir into the creamed mixture alternately with the soaked fruit.

Pour into a greased and lined baking tin and bake at 140°C (275°C/Gas Mark 1) for about 2½ hours, or until the top is brown and the sides begin to shrink away from the tin.

Leave until cold before storing. If liked, when cold, prick the top and pour over 1 tablespoon of brandy before storing.

Madeira Cake

This firm sponge cake makes a good base for decorating. It is an alternative to fruit cake mixtures, and can be used for a sponge layer in a wedding cake. The mixture will make a 18cm (7in) round cake or a 15cm (6in) square.

100g (4oz/½ cup) butter
100g (4oz/½ cup) sugar
2 medium-sized eggs
100g (4oz/1 cup) self-raising flour
25g (1oz/¼ cup) plain (all-purpose) flour
50g (2oz/½ cup) ground almonds
juice of a medium-sized lemon

Cream the butter and sugar until light and fluffy. Beat the eggs together and gradually beat into the creamed mixture.

Sift together the flours and ground almonds. Fold into the creamed mixture together with the lemon juice.

Pour into a greased baking tin and bake at 160°C (325°F/Gas Mark 3) for 40 minutes, or until risen and golden brown on top and firm to the touch.

Swiss Roll (Jelly Roll)

These cakes can be placed side by side and iced to give an unusual base for celebration cakes. This mixture makes one roll. Use a 25 x 35cm (10 x 14in) Swiss roll tin or shallow baking pan.

3 medium-sized eggs
100g (4oz/½ cup) sugar, warmed
65g (2½oz/⅔ cup) self-raising flour, sifted

Put the eggs in a heatproof bowl, add the warmed sugar and beat with an electric mixer until the mixture is foamy and double in bulk.

Using a metal spoon, gently fold in the flour. Prepare the tin or pan by brushing it with oil and lining with a piece of oiled greaseproof or wax paper. Spread the mixture evenly.

Bake at 220°C (425°F/Gas Mark 7) for 10-12 minutes, or until lightly brown and springy to the touch. Turn out the warm cake on a piece of greaseproof or wax paper lightly dusted with cornflour (cornstarch).

If filling with jam, spread warmed jam evenly over the surface, trim the long sides, roll up and leave until cold.

If filling with buttercream, trim the long sides and roll up around a piece of greaseproof or wax paper. Leave until cold, then gently unroll, fill with buttercream and reroll.

Designing a Cake

When designing a cake, the first thing to consider is for what occasion the cake is to be used. If decorating a cake for a children's party or for elderly people, it is best to avoid any decoration that is not edible.

The next thing to think of is the number of people the cake must serve. This will determine the size of the cake and the number of tiers. There may be occasions when people want a small, tiered wedding cake. In this case, all decorations have to be reduced in size. A small cake will be overwhelmed by large flowers, so everything must be miniaturized.

The next decision is about colour: which colours will combine best with the overall design. Get colour samples or fresh flowers to work from, particularly if strong colours are to be used.

Consider the proportions and balance of the design. There are many books describing the rules and regulations for this. However, fashion does change, and ideas with it. The best guide is your eye, together with these few basic guidelines.

Traditionally, royal-iced cakes have a graduation of 5cm (2in) between tiers, and it has also been traditional that the depth of the top tier is less than that of the bottom tier. However, if a cake is covered in sugarpaste, it is usual to have a 7.5cm (3in) differential in tier size, and the depth of all the tiers is the same. If supporting the tiers with pillars, those on a royal-iced cake can decrease in height, while pillars on a sugarpasted cake must be the same height.

The board for the lowest tier of a cake can be proportionately larger than the boards of the upper tiers. The boards in a tiered cake should be the same size as the cake in the layer immediately below. If using a vase of sugar flowers on the top of a cake, have the tiers graduated in 5cm (2in) sizes. This creates a more attractively proportioned cake than the usual 7.5cm (3in) graduations.

When designing a tiered cake with embroidery and lace, keep in mind the depths of the cakes. If decreasing the depth of each tier, the lace and embroidery designs must be decreased in the same proportions or the designs will look very heavy on the smallest tier. When designing scallops for a three-tier cake, it is easier to match a design by dividing it into three when starting to work.

Before beginning to decorate a cake, have a mental picture of what it should look like when finished. Draw it so that you have something to refer to while decorating. Remember, though, that sometimes when working on a cake a different pattern may start to emerge. If it looks good, follow it, even if it is not the design originally planned. Instinct plays a great part in creativity, and new ideas are continually being sought by enthusiastic cake decorators.

Design for fuchsia brush embroidery

Fuchsia Wedding Cake
This perfectly-designed three-tiered wedding cake incorporates fuchsias in the lace and embroidery patterns. The bottom tier is a 30cm (12in) round sugarpasted cake, with the other tiers in proportion. The unusual cake stand is covered with wired sugar ivy.

14

Royal Icing

Good royal icing is the beginning of an exquisitely decorated cake. It is probably the most commonly used icing, whether for coating a cake in the English fashion, piping, collars, delicate embroidery, lace or tulle work, elaborate filigree or pretty run-outs. It is so versatile that some decorators use no other icing, although most prefer to combine it with other icings or coverings. The royal-iced cake here has fine Oriental stringwork and is topped with a tulle butterfly.

Working with Royal Icing

Basic Royal Icing

2-3 large egg whites, which have been exposed to the air for 24 hours to liquify

450g (1lb) icing (confectioner's) sugar, sifted

Put the egg whites in a bowl. Gradually stir in half of the icing sugar until the mixture is the consistency of unwhipped cream. Add the rest of the icing sugar, a spoonful at a time, stirring after each addition. Stir, do not beat, the icing, until it reaches the desired consistency. There should be firm peaks when a wooden spatula is withdrawn from the icing.

If using an electric mixer, mix the egg whites on the lowest speed for a maximum of four minutes, then add the sugar as above. The electric mixer method produces a lot of air bubbles, so the icing must be left for 24 hours before use to allow the air bubbles to come to the surface and burst. With both methods, scrape down the sides of the bowl and cover the icing with clingfilm. Cover the bowl with a damp cloth and put a plate on the top to prevent the icing from crusting.

Note: Royal icing can be made from powdered egg albumen, which is usually obtainable from cake decorating shops. Use according to the manufacturer's instructions. This produces a whiter icing than that made from fresh eggs, but the icing is not suitable for stringwork or extension work.

Coating a cake

Place the marzipanned cake on a board, and put a quantity of royal icing on top. With a straight knife or palette knife, spread the icing evenly across the surface of the cake and paddle the icing backwards and forwards, at the same time rotating the turntable, so that the air bubbles come to the surface and burst.

Holding the knife at a 45° angle to the surface and holding the board with your other hand, rotate the turntable in one continuous movement to spread the icing evenly across the surface.

Remove the cake from the turntable. Hold a metal straight edge level at a 45° angle to the surface of the cake. Draw the ruler towards you carefully and evenly. Do not press too hard with the first coat. Return the surplus icing to the bowl and clean the straight edge. Remove any icing from the side of cake and allow top coat to dry.

Return the cake to the turntable. Spread more icing evenly down the sides with the knife by using a paddling motion while rotating the turntable. Holding the scraper at a slight angle to the cake, revolve the turntable smoothly and fairly quickly in one continuous movement with the other hand. When the cake has been turned completely, gradually draw off the scraper. This will leave a slight 'take off' mark. Remove all icing from the cake board. Leave until dry.

When the cake is completely dry, remove any rough edges with a very sharp knife or fine sandpaper. Remove any loose particles of icing from the cake.

For subsequent coats, the icing should be of a slightly softer consistency. There should be at least two coats of royal icing, but a wedding cake would normally have three or four coats. The icing must be dry before decorating.

Coating the board
Coat the board with a thin layer of icing. Holding the knife almost flat, rotate the board to smooth the surface. Holding the knife at a 45° angle, rotate the turntable and bevel the edge of the icing. Clean any surplus icing from the side of the board.

Icing Bags

Icing bags are best made from good quality greaseproof paper, which is inexpensive. Greaseproof paper is obtainable in sheets 38 x 25cm (15 x 10in) or in rolls. It is easier to use the sheets, as they are already cut to a convenient size.

Never make a bag larger than is necessary for the job in hand. Should you put too much icing in the bag, it puts an unnecessary strain on your hand, resulting in unsteady work. Also, the heat from your hand will tend to make the sugar dry out, causing frequent breaks when piping.

Large bag: For star tubes and tubes with a large aperture, fold the sheet of greaseproof paper diagonally.
Small bag: For plain tubes, petal and leaf tubes, with a small aperture, fold the sheet of greaseproof paper in half before folding diagonally.

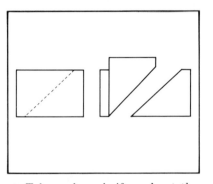

1 Take a sharp knife and cut the paper along the folded edge, producing two large bag shapes from each rectangular piece, or four small bag shapes.

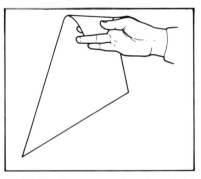

2 Hold the paper in the right hand, so that the right angle is on the right-hand side and the short edge is at the top.

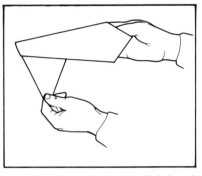

3 Take the point in the left hand and bring this upwards and over the right hand. Do not pull tight, but allow it to remain slack.

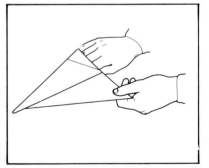

4 Turn the right hand anti-clockwise (counter-clockwise) and at the same time move the left hand point towards the right hand until a sharp point is obtained and the bag becomes taut.

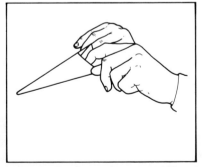

5 If making small bags, withdraw the third and fourth fingers of the right hand so that the bag will not be too wide at the top when completed. Transfer the point to the thumb and forefinger of the right hand temporarily, without letting the bag unroll, then turn the bag until the point is facing away from you.

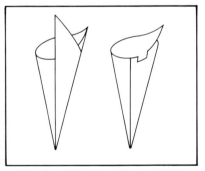

6 Fold in the flap once and then again. Make two small tears approximately 5mm (¼in) apart, and fold the flap down to lock in position.

Run-outs

Make up royal icing to the usual consistency. If colouring the icing do it now. Leave enough in the bowl to fill a small bag. Place the icing in a separate bowl and add more egg white, a little at a time, stirring with a wooden spatula. Hold the spatula up and allow the icing to fall into the bowl. It should find its own level by the count of ten. If it is too stiff, add a little more egg white; if too runny, add a little more royal icing.

When the right consistency is reached, cover with a damp cloth, and bang the bowl on a towel for about a half a minute to allow the air bubbles to come to the surface. Leave covered with a damp cloth for about 30 minutes. The air bubbles will rise to the surface, where they can be cut with a spatula.

1 Begin at the back of the picture. Fill a piping bag and cut off the tip to represent a No2 piping tube. Flood in the face and with a fine paintbrush ease the icing to the edge of the outline and back over the hairline. With a No0 tube pipe the stem. Flood the shoe, the back ribbon and alternate layers on the dress.

2 Flood the front of the dress to the first layer. Flood the remaining layers. With stiff royal icing pipe the hair, bringing it over the face and building it up to the required thickness.

Collars

Thin the remaining royal icing with a little water for use with a No 1 tube. Cut out a piece of wax paper a little larger than the collar. Press the wax paper firmly with your fingernail outside the design so that it will stick to the design without having to put any royal icing under the corners.

Have a small bag with a No1 tube and all the large bags ready before you begin to pipe the collar. From a height, pour the run-out icing into a large bag without a nozzle, to break any remaining air bubbles.

Pipe the outline of the collar with a No1 tube. Always start piping from the inside. When you have piped the outline remove the wax paper from the design and place it onto a piece of plate glass, placing a little royal icing under the corners of the wax paper to stick it to the glass.

Run-out figures

Roll out a plaque of sugarpaste 2mm (⅛in) thick. The edge can be left plain or crimped. Leave to dry on a wooden board.

With a 2B pencil trace the picture onto tracing paper. Turn the tracing over and trace over the original outline on the back. Turn the picture over again and place on the plaque. With an HB pencil trace over the outline again.

Mix the royal icing as for the run-out collars but use water instead of egg white to thin down the icing. Each layer of icing should skin before the next one is added.

3 Pipe a bulb of icing in the centre of the hand and use a fine paintbrush to gently stroke the icing to the fingertips and back under the sleeve. Flood the hat, making certain it covers the ends of the hair.

4 Flood the band around the hat and the other ribbon. Flood the sleeve and leave to dry. Outline the details with a very fine paintbrush and add small flowers to the stem.

Floating Collars

In this technique, fine strands of royal icing are used to support the uppermost collar above the cake, giving the appearance that it is floating. The piping is similar to extension work.

The cake shown here is 18cm (7in). Place it on a 30cm (12in) board and coat with white royal icing. Use the templates to pipe the top collar and floating collar following the instructions on page 20.

Make a template for the bottom collar, and cut the inside circle large enough to place around the iced cake on the board. Pipe the outline of the template with a No1 tube then remove the template and flood the bottom collar.

Fill a large bag with thick royal icing and cut to represent a No2 nozzle. Pipe a band around the top of the cake and position the top collar. With a No1 tube, pipe a circle on the cake 1mm (1/20in) from the inside edge of the collar. Pipe a second circle 1mm (1/20in) inside the first. Overpipe both with a No0.

Cut six wooden blocks 2cm (3/4in) square and 5cm (2in) long. Position as shown and place the floating collar on top of them. With a No00 tube, pipe evenly spaced extensions. Pipe from the base upwards on the inside, and from the top down on the outside. Work one section at a time, removing the blocks as soon as the icing is dry.

Decorate the top edge of the collar with picot dots. Overpipe the base collar with a No1 tube, then overpipe with a No0. Come in with a No0. Pipe small dots to join the cake and base collar.

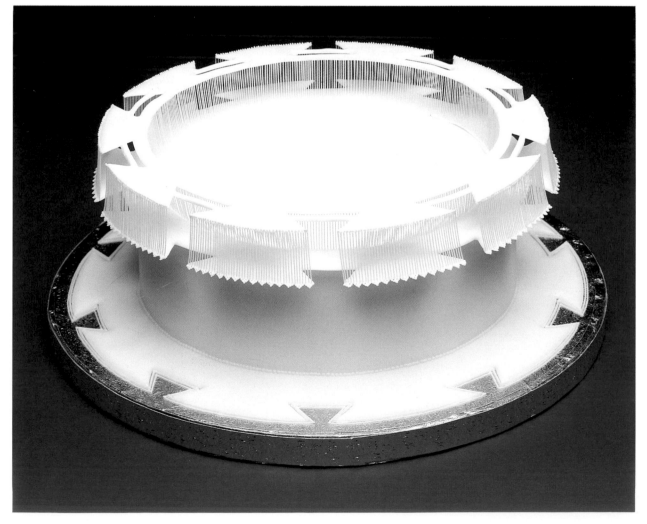

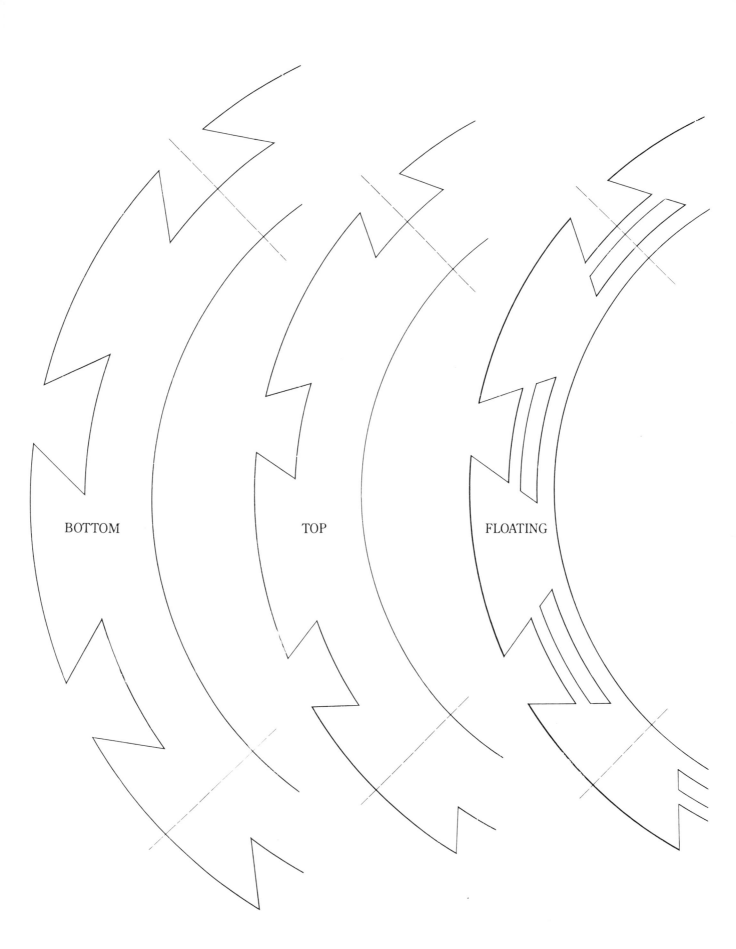

BOTTOM

TOP

FLOATING

¼ of each template is between the broken lines.

Oriental Stringwork

This technique produces exquisitely delicate results. However, because the cake must be handled more than with most other decorating techniques, use a firm-textured fruit cake rather than a light sponge cake.

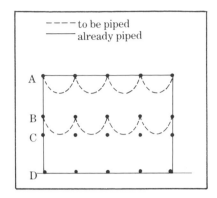

Oriental Stringwork Icing

1 egg white
225-280g (8-10oz/2-2¼ cups) icing (confectioner's) sugar
0.5ml (⅛ teaspoon) gum arabic or gum acacia
1ml (¼ teaspoon) liquid glucose

Mix following the method for royal icing on page 12, adding the gum arabic or acacia and liquid glucose after the icing sugar has been incorporated.

Colour as required.

The template and diagrams on this page are for the Oriental stringwork cake shown on page 16, and illustrate the basic technique. The cake is 18cm (7in). Place on a 23cm (9in) round board and coat with pale lilac royal icing. Stringwork icing is purple and white.

This cake shows a slightly more complicated variation of Oriental stringwork, but it is still done using the techniques described.

1 Use the template to position 20 dots of purple royal icing on the top edge of the cake. Place a set square vertically against the cake and mark the other three rows as shown. Using a No0 tube and purple icing, drop loops from dot to dot in rows A and B. The loops should be about 1.5cm (½in) deep.

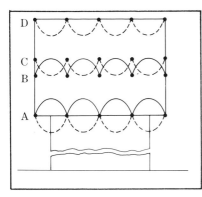

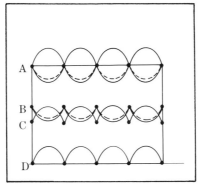

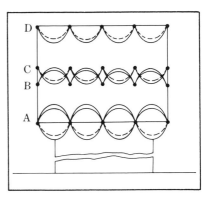

2 Carefully turn the cake over. Place a firm, tall support with a diameter smaller than that of the cake on top and turn them so that the cake rests on the support. Pipe loops along rows D, C and A. Turn the cake upright.

3 Using the white icing, pipe a smaller row of loops along rows A and B. Each loop should start and finish in the centre of a dot, and they should build out to give a three-dimensional effect. Do not pipe all the loops in one direction at the same time, as this destroys the interleaving look.

4 Turn the cake over and pipe white loops along rows D, C and A. Turn the cake upright and pipe smaller loops along rows A and B. Continue in this way, making smaller loops and alternating colours until there are three layers of loops in the middle and five layers at the top and bottom. When dry, position small flowers over the dots, if wished.

Tulle Work

This unusual technique involves piping royal icing onto tulle to produce delicate decorations. It is most successful when bride's tulle or bridal veiling is used, as net is rarely fine enough. Tulle work can be used to produce a variety of lovely designs.

Basic tulle piping

These instructions are for the tulle butterfly, but the method of tulle piping is the same for all of the objects on these pages. Place the template on a flat polystyrene tile or cakeboard and cover with a larger piece of wax paper. Cut the tulle to the correct shape and pin tautly over the template. Using a No00 tube, start piping from the inside. Pipe the outside edge with a No0 tube. Finish the edges with a snails trail. When dry, turn over and pipe the other side. Pipe each piece separately.

To assemble the butterfly when tulle wings are dry, pipe the head and body with a No2 tube and stiff royal icing. Press two stamens into the head for antennae. Gently press the wings in position and prop with sponge or tissue until dry. Add details with a very fine paint brush.

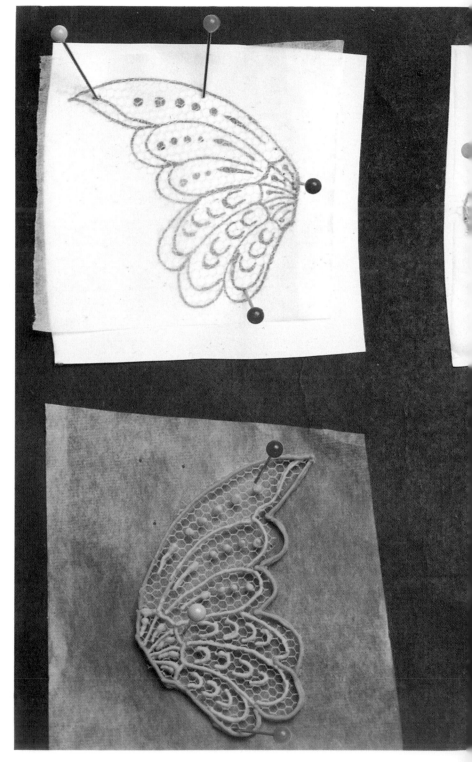

Tulle Gazebo

Cut the base and the round plinth from modelling paste. When dry, stick base over plinth with royal icing.

Make three side panels and the two front panels following instructions for tulle piping. When dry, use a No3 bag and thick royal icing to stick each piece to the base and to the adjacent pieces.

Pipe six roof sections. When dry, stick one section to the top of a side panel. Attach the opposite side piece and build up this way. Put a bulb of royal icing in the middle.

Pipe lace pieces and attach to bottom of base. Decorate with tiny flowers and leaves.

Christmas tree
Use the template to cut one piece of tulle, then cut four half trees without the top star. Follow instructions for tulle piping. When the pieces are dry, assemble by carefully attaching the half pieces to the main body with thick royal icing. Pipe snowflakes onto wax paper with a No00 tube, and attach to points of tree as shown.

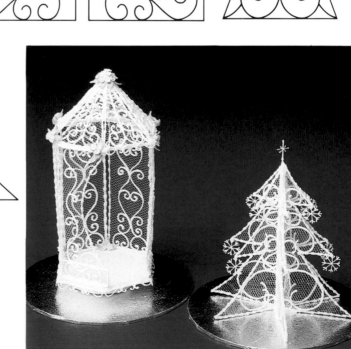

Pagoda-roofed Gazebo

Cut the three sections for the base from modelling paste. When dry, stick together with royal icing with the smallest piece at the top.

Pipe five side pieces using the same template as for the Tulle Gazebo. Pipe the door. When dry, attach to the base and to each other with thick royal icing.

Pipe six roof sections and leave to dry over a piece of 16cm (6¼in) tube to create a slight curve. Attach as for the other gazebo. Finish the top with a swirl of royal icing.

Pipe lace pieces and attach to bottom of base. Decorate with tiny flowers and leaves. The gazebos can be used as free-standing ornaments or as elegant cake-top decorations.

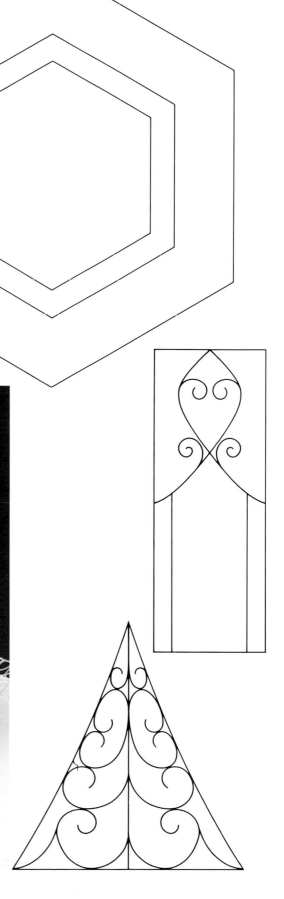

Tulle Extension Work

This technique uses tulle piping to create a delicate, lacy border around the base of a cake.

Choose the design you wish to use. It is best to have a shallow scallop at the base, and a sharp point at the upper edge. Finish off the lower edge of the cake with a shell, snailstrail or ribbon banding.

Cut out the template to be used on a band of greaseproof paper, and mark the design onto the side of the cake with a pin or a scriber. Take one scallop from the design and cut a piece of tulle slightly broader than the design drawn on the cake. The length should be the same. Pin this on to the cake at the three points of the design and see that you have a good fit. There should be a good curve at the base of the design, and the side edges should fit neatly.

Once you have established the best shape for the pieces, check to see how many pieces you need and cut the appropriate number. Pin each individual piece to the cake with glass-headed pins so that there is a continuous design going around the cake. Pipe a fine snailstrail onto the outer edge of the pieces, fastening them to the side of the cake. Pipe a snailstrail along the lower edge of each scallop. Now pipe cornelli work or a similar design over the pieces so that they harden off and form a firm decorative border to the cake. Remove the pins and finish the design of the cake as planned. This can include a band of embroidery, lace pieces or sugar flowers.

Posy Cake
*Position a 23cm (9in) round cake
on a 28cm (11in) board and coat
with pale green sugarpaste.
Position ribbon banding and bows
and embossing before doing the
tulle extension work as described
here. The cake is finished with a
posy, trimmed with matching
ribbons.*

Heart Engagement Cake
This exquisite heart-shaped cake would be perfect for an engagement party or for a small wedding. The lace pattern and brush embroidery both feature bleeding hearts, which are also included in the crescent spray.

Fuchsia lace

Bleeding heart lace

Wedding bell lace

Lace

Lace is used on many cakes. As with extension work, it is best done with freshly made royal icing and piped with a No0 or 00 tube.

Calculate how many pieces you will need. This should be easy as lace pieces are usually designed as divisions of an inch (2.5cm). Pipe several extra lace pieces to allow for breakages. The neatest and most attractive way of fastening the lace pieces to the cake is to attach them with two small dots of royal icing.

Once the lace piece is fastened to the cake you can adjust the angle by using a fine, dry paint brush.

To pipe lace, place a piece of wax paper or roasting wrap onto a piece of glass or perspex and fasten with masking tape. Follow the design carefully, eliminating bulbs or twists in the icing. Remove any

marks or flaws with a very fine, damp sable brush. When the icing has set, gently loosen the lace pieces with a fine, dry sable brush or with a fine-bladed crank-handled palette knife. It is important to use a crank-handled palette knife as it can be positioned flat against the glass, making breakages less likely.

Extension Work

Extension work is also called 'curtain borders', and is one of the more difficult techniques. A cake decorator should be comfortable using No0 and No00 tubes before attempting this work.

If you plan to include extension work on a cake, place the cake on a larger board than usual so you don't accidentally break the icing.

The coating on the cake should be a few days old before doing the extension work. To transfer the pattern to the cake, take a piece of greaseproof paper the same depth as the cake, and 1.5cm (½in) longer than the circumference of the cake. Wrap around the cake, overlap the join and tape it down. Remove and fold the band into as many segments as you want. Draw the design on the top segment. It is usual to have the bottom edge of the scallops about 2.5-3cm (1-1½in) long.

Next, consider how long the drop should be. It is usual to have it between one-half and one-third the depth of the cake. Choose the design for the upper edge. The simplest pattern is a straight line from which the threads drop. The straight line is most easily achieved using a pair of dividers. Set one arm on the board, and the other to the height of the line. Gently make the line. A scalloped upper edge gives a more interesting design.

Cut the pattern on the folded piece of greaseproof paper, and mark it onto the cake using a scriber, darning needle or similar object. Insert a No0 tube into a bag, fill with a little royal icing and carefully pipe a snailstrail around the lower edge of the cake. The scallops for the bridgework should come about 5mm (¼in) above the board. Do not allow the bridge to touch the board.

If you are going to have embroidery, ribbon insertion or broiderie anglaise on the cake above the extension work, do it before you start on the bridge work. If you want decorations such as pictures or appliquéd flowers on the side of the cake behind the extension work, apply them now. Be careful not to touch the places where the scallops or the upper edge of the drop threads will be.

Decide on the shape of the bridge. The extension work can form a smooth, continuous line, or a wavy one.

Before starting on the bridge, lift the cake to a comfortable height so that you are piping at eye level. Make sure you are working in very good light. It may also help to lift the back of the cake slightly so that the loops will drop a little more easily.

Bridge Work

Method 1 Using a bag with a No0 tube, drop the first layer of bridge against the side of the cake, keeping the scallops as even as possible. There must not be any gaps between the surface of the cake and

---

Royal Icing for Extension Work

white of 1 large egg, string removed

175-190g (7-7½oz/1¾-2 cups) icing sugar

pinch of tartaric acid (cream of tartar)

Place the egg white in the bowl of an electric mixer and carefully sift in the icing sugar through a fine-meshed sieve. Add the tartaric acid. Cover the bowl and turn the mixer to the slowest speed. When all the icing sugar has been combined with the egg white, turn the speed to low and beat for 4-8 minutes, or until full peak is reached. The right consistency is very important: only experience will tell you when you have reached the correct peak.

When filling a bag for any fine piping work, always place a small piece of nylon stocking inside the bag. Spoon in the icing, grasp the stocking firmly, force the icing through it, and remove and discard the stocking. This removes any undissolved specks of icing sugar, sugar granules or air bubbles from the icing.

Christening Cake
Delicate extension work is featured on this feminine Christening cake. The royal-iced 25cm (10in) long oval is positioned on a 33cm (13in) board. Instructions for making the filigree pram are on page 42. Add the bootees and pipe the baby's name on the cake if wished.

the bridge, or there will be weak spots in the bridge. Keep a very damp cloth to wipe the tip of the tube before starting the next drop. This bit of moisture in the tip of the tube will help the icing stick to the previous loop. Use a very fine, damp sable brush to touch any loose sections of icing into place. Go all the way around the cake before starting the next layer of the bridge. Each layer should be dry before starting the next stage.

Drop the next line immediately over the previous one. The starting point of each layer must be in the same place. Do not start a loop with a bulb: keep it all as fine as possible. When looking at the bridge work from the side you should not be able to see any lines but the last one you piped into place – the bridge work must not develop a scooped look.

It is usual to bring the bridging out seven lines if using a No1 tube, and 14 lines if using a No0. If there are a few weaknesses in the bridge, use run-out consistency royal icing and a bag with a small hole cut in it to gently coat the bridge. Use a fine brush to spread the icing evenly, filling in any gaps or weak spots. Leave this to dry before starting the drop lines.

Remove the prop which has been tilting the the cake, and start piping the drop lines. Start at the base tier and work upwards. The secret of accurate drop lines is to have them as close together as possible. You must not be able to fit another drop line in the spaces. Pipe directly in front of the cake. Turn it slightly after every two or three lines, or some lines may fall at an angle.

To ensure straight lines, pipe a tiny spot of icing, touch it to the cake and draw the thread down and outwards, taking the thread below the bridge work before allowing it to touch the bridge and become fastened to it. Carefully trim off any short excess strands with a damp, fine sable brush. Do not stop the piping on the bridge.

The easiest way to finish off the work is to use the same tube used for the drop lines. Touch the tube to the highest point of a scallop and drop a line covering the bottom of the drop lines where they join the bridge.

Another method is to pipe a very fine snailstrail over the spot where the drop lines meet the bridge. Pipe very tiny loops from drop thread to drop thread, or pipe from every

other thread as for Oriental stringwork. This can be varied in many ways to create fascinating patterns. A picot edge can be attractive. This is a series of small pearls piped next to each other but not quite touching. The first row is three pearls and a gap, three pearls and a gap, etc. The next layer consists of two small pearls piped in the spaces between the first three, and the last layer is a single pearl piped between the two of the previous layer.

Method II Start the bridge as before, piping all around the cake. Pipe the next layer on to the first layer, but start the line just short of the top of the scallop and finish it before you reach the next apex. Repeat this for each layer of bridge work. Start the final layer at the top of a scallop, going over all the previously shortened pieces.

To ensure that the lower edge is smooth, pipe two full layers from one apex to the other. Drop the lines as for Method I, and finish off in one of the ways described. You can also drop a series of loops from one bridge to the next, increasing them slightly in size to create a cobweb effect.

It is possible to pipe onto the individual threads of the drop lines. The most common way is hail spotting: piping a series of tiny, even dots down one thread of the extension work. On the next thread, pipe dots which fit into the gaps between those previously piped. This is repeated along every thread. A steady hand is needed for this work. Another design is to pipe tiny forget-me-nots and leaves onto the threads, creating an attractive pattern. This is particularly pretty when done in a contrasting or toning colour.

Double extension work: Complete the bridge work and the drop lines as described. Instead of finishing off, start again on a second layer of bridgework, exactly in the same position as the first, layering it on top of the finishing points in the first layer of drop lines. The second bridge should have the same number of lines as the first one. Start the drop lines a bit above those of the previous layer. Finish off as desired.

Double extension work is more effective if the drop lines are coloured for the first layer and white for the second layer.

Curtain extension work: Complete

the extension work up to the drop lines. Pipe another two layers of bridge work. Using either a tilting turntable or a prop, tilt the cake slightly. Drop a second layer of drop lines onto the new bridge, working from the centre to the outer edge of the scallop. Continue all around the cake in one direction. When the layer is complete, tilt the cake in the opposite direction and repeat the process, working around the cake. This is particularly effective if the second layer is in a deeper colour than the first layer of drop lines. The central background can be decorated with embroidered flowers.

Pointed extension work: This style is different in that the scallops are pointed rather than rounded. The resulting bridgework leaves areas at the base of the cake exposed, creating an unusual effect.

Transfer the pattern to the cake. Attach a narrow band of ribbon around the cake at the base, and pipe a snailstrail. Insert embroidery in the gaps where the design has been lifted.

Pipe the bridge with the cake tilted so that it is more like built-up line work than the usual dropped scallops. Pipe the drop lines as usual.

Tiered extension work: This is a technique for the very experienced. The extension work is built up in two or three separate sections. Mark the design onto the cake. Pipe the snailstrail. Pipe the first layer of bridge work and drop lines. When this is dry, drop the second layer of bridge lines immediately above the upper edge of the first layer of drop lines.

Another idea for the very experienced is to design the pattern with scallops at both the upper and lower edges of the cake. Mark the design onto the cake as usual, and pipe the bridge. Tilt the cake forward and use a No0 or 00 tube to pipe a loop so that it drops away from the side of the cake. Fill in the scallop above the loop with a series of smaller loops to create delicate cobwebs. Allow this to dry and continue working in the same way all around the cake. When this is finished, pipe the drop lines from the loop to the bridge work.

It is traditional for the upper layer of extension work to be finished off with a fine layer of lace. Use a small design that does not overpower the extension work.

These illustrations show different styles of extension work: basic extension work with different lace; double extension work; pointed extension work; tiered extension work. Using a second colour makes an intersting contrast. The very experienced decorator could experiment by doing extension work in several different colours.

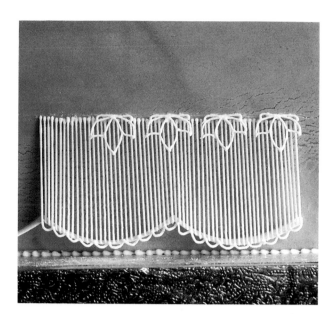

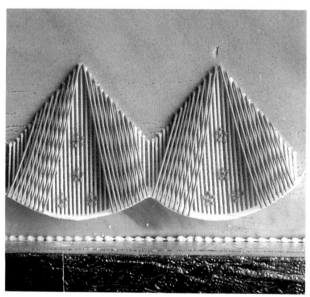

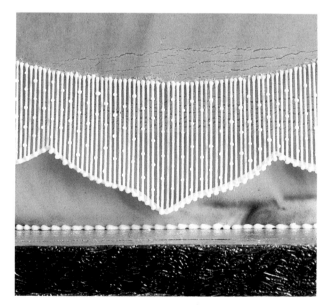

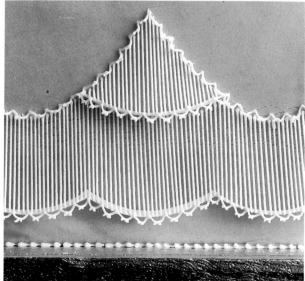

Embroidery and Brush Embroidery

There are many sources of inspiration for embroidery designs. Look on clothing, lace, needlework or in books. Brush embroidery is a method for creating pictures using a piping tube and a fine sable brush.

Embroidery

The icing for embroidery should be made to a soft peak consistency. Force the icing through a piece of nylon stocking as you put it in the bag. Do not overfill the bag. Two to three teaspoons of icing should be sufficient to complete the embroidery decoration on a whole cake. Embroidery is usually done with a No0 tube.

An experienced decorator should be able to do embroidery freehand onto the cake. However, it is quite easy to mark the design onto the cake. Draw the design onto the greaseproof paper used to mark extension or other work, and carefully prick the main guidepoints onto the cake through the paper. Try practising the embroidery on a sugarpaste plaque and work on the side of a coated dummy to learn the difference between piping downwards, and piping onto the side of a cake. Learn to work on a small scale by piping onto mint creams, sugared almonds or sugar cubes.

If planning to include embroidery designs on tiered cakes, the designs must be ones which can successfully be reduced. A design that looks good on a single tier may look very odd when repeated several times. Also be careful not to transpose a design.

When piping an all-over design spread it evenly, as any discrepancy will be obvious. One way to ensure accuracy when the sugarpaste is still soft is to draw a grid on a paper cut-out of the top of the cake. Ice the meeting points of the guidelines on to a piece of glass or perspex with full peak consistency icing and a No0 tube. The design should be situated at the meeting points. Allow the icing to dry, invert the dry icing points onto the soft surface of the cake, lining up the edges carefully, and gently press the icing onto the cake, leaving small marks. To mark designs on a royal-iced cake use masking tape, which will hold the design firmly in place without marking the surface.

Brush embroidery

Use freshly made royal icing at full peak, but to each four tablespoons of icing add one teaspoon of clear piping jel. This will slow down drying and allow a longer time to work on the design without the icing crusting.

Put the icing into two bags, one with a No0 tube and the other with a No1. Fine detail can later be added with a No00 tube, if necessary. Work in the same colour as the cake coating, or in contrasting colours. If working in the base colour, delicately tint the finished, dry design with petal dust.

Transfer the design to the surface of the cake. Using a No0 tube start work on the background. Pipe the first outline. If it is to be delicate, pipe a second, finer line inside the first. With a fine sable brush and a little water, gently smooth the icing from the outer edge of the design towards the centre. Do not stop half way; bring each brush stroke into the centre, leaving a fine film of sugar over the whole surface of the design. Leave a line around the edge of the design. If necessary, add a little more icing where it is needed. Continue in this way until the design is completed.

Keep the various textures of the picture clearly in mind. Observe the veins and markings on leaves and petals and copy them. Veins on leaves can be emphasised either by overpiping, or by removing the icing completely with the fine point of a paint brush.

If working in colour be sure to get the icing in the right place, as removing it may leave stains. Put any shading in very delicately, keeping in mind the direction from which the light is coming.

Design for embroidery

Design for bleeding heart brush embroidery

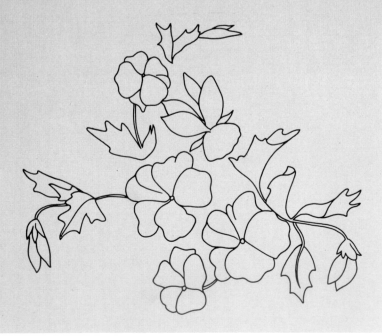

Embroidered Pansy Cake
*Pansies feature in this special
occasion cake, both in the floral
spray and in the delicately coloured
brush embroidery. The embroidery
pattern is shown below. Finish the
brush embroidery before beginning
the fine pointed extension work.*

Tube Embroidery

This technique involves piping with No00, 0 or 1 tubes with several colours of icing. You need a tube containing every colour in the design, which means having many tubes of the same size. You will need a jar of water, a fine sable brush and a damp cloth to keep the tube tips moist.

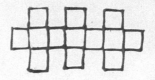

Running: Pipe with short, even strokes along the line of the design. Leave small gaps between the strokes.

Feather: Pipe a tiny U-shaped stroke. Start the next U-shape just inside the base of the previous one.

Faggot (Holbein): Pipe a series of short strokes to form neat squares.

Backstitch: Pipe short, even strokes one behind the other so that they just touch, tapering the ends.

Lazy Daisy: Pipe a series of small, open teardrops. Pipe in the holding stitch at the broad end.

Crosstitch: Pipe crosses next to each other.

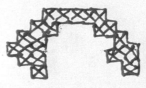

Herringbone: Pipe a tiny teardrop, tapering towards the centre. Pipe another teardrop, starting on the opposite side of the central line.

Long and short: Pipe a series of long and short strokes next to each other.

Assisi work: Pipe the outlines, then complete with crosstitch.

Stemstitch: Pipe tiny strokes along the design line. Each stroke starts alongside the previous stroke, slightly underneath it.

Satin: Pipe a series of straight lines next to each other and at an angle. For padded satin, pipe satin stitch over a smooth layer of royal icing.

Byzantine (Florentine): Pipe a series of long and short strokes.

Chainstitch: Pipe a small teardrop, and use a damp, fine sable brush to gently open the centre. Pipe the next teardrop starting just inside the previous stitch.

Algerian eye stitch: Pipe a series of straight strokes to form a spoked wheel. Do not cross the spokes. Finish with a tiny dot piped in the centre.

Knots: Pipe small circles of icing with finishing strokes emerging from the centre.

Filigree Work

Delicate, lacy filigree piping can be used to make gorgeous decorations, such as the tiny pram, on this feminine christening cake. For best results, use fresh royal icing made following the instructions for extension work icing.

Piping the pieces

Trace all of the pieces for the pram from the templates. Piece K is a guide to show the position of the wheels.

Pipe the base (A) on wax paper placed over a piece of plastic tube with a 5.5cm (2⅛in) diameter. Pipe the hood (B) on wax paper over a 4.3cm (1¹¹⁄₁₆in) tube. The shade sides (C and D), pram sides (E and F), four wheels (G and H), and the handle bar (J) are piped flat onto wax paper.

Use a No0 tube to pipe the outline of A, B, C, D, E and F, then pipe the diagonal trellis work with a 0 or 00. Pipe the wheels with a No0.

When the trellis work is dry, pipe the flower pattern on the pram sides and shade sides. Overpipe all the parts of the pattern pieces that are drawn with broken lines in the templates.

Assembling the pram

Place E flat and, holding A, pipe a line of icing around the curve. Lay A onto E and leave to dry. Assemble B and C in the same way.

Lay F flat and, holding the two pieces already assembled, pipe around the curve. Place A and E onto F and leave to dry. Attach B and C to D in the same way.

Lay the pram on its side. Attach the small wheels to the shade end and the large wheels at the handle end. Use K as a guide to the correct positions. Make sure all four wheels are level. Turn the pram upsidedown on a small block of wood while the wheels dry. The handle should come over the side of the block and not touch anything.

Pipe a line of icing around the bottom of the shade and attach to the pram. Attach the handle bars with small dots of icing piped onto the side handle pieces.

If wished, neaten the seams by piping teardrops with a No00 tube.

A

J

B

C   D

E

F

G

H

K

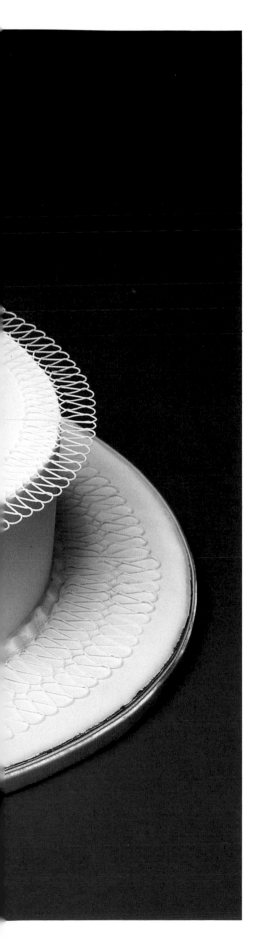

Bride and Groom Cake

This unusual wedding cake uses several techniques – tulle work, filigree, and different piping methods. If preferred, the bride and groom can be used as a free-standing table decoration.

To make the filigree-collared cake, place a 25cm (10in) cake on a 38cm (15in) board and coat both with white royal icing.

Use the templates to pipe the six top and six bottom collar pieces onto wax paper. Pipe with a No0 tube, making certain that all the points touch for strength. For greater strength, pipe the top collar with Oriental stringwork icing (see page 24). Dry on plate glass, then remove from wax paper.

Pipe a shell edge around the base of the cake with a No43 tube.

Position the bottom collar with the inside edge just touching the soft icing. Attach a velvet ribbon around the edge of the board.

Attach the top collar with royal icing and a No0 tube. Centre the bride and groom and attach with a little thick royal icing.

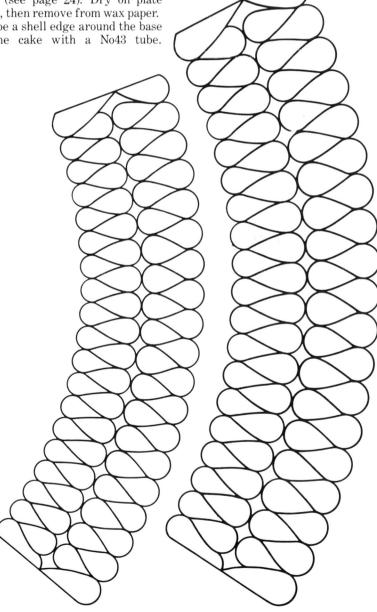

Bride

Cut a piece of tulle for the veil as shown on the template. Place the main body design on the tile and the other pieces on plate glass. Cover with a larger piece of wax paper. Press the wax paper firmly with your fingernail around the outside edge of the design. Pin the tulle to the board in the correct position.

Pipe the detail with a No00 and outline the edges with a No0 tube. Overpipe the sleeve for greater depth. Strengthen all the joins with a snailstrail. Leave to dry completely. Remove the bride from the wax paper and turn it over on a black background. Pipe the other side for greater strength.

Groom

Make as for the bride, but without the tulle. For the stripe on the trousers, pipe two parallel straight lines with a No0 tube, then pressure pipe the centre to fill in. Overpipe the bottom of the jacket. When completely dry turn over and pipe the reverse side.

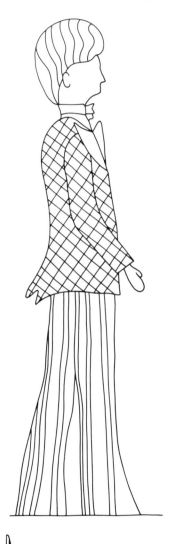

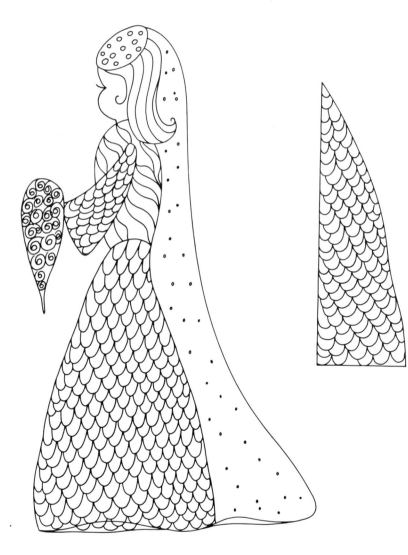

Base

Cut out two flower paste circles, 11cm (4½in) and 10cm (4in), When dry, place a 1.5cm (½in) thick ring of flower paste on the larger circle and moisten with a little egg white to stick the circles together.

Using a No0 or No00 tube and royal icing, drop 5mm (¼in) loops evenly around the edge of the top circle. When dry, carefully turn the base over and stand it on a firm, tall support with a smaller diameter. Drop loops evenly around the base, matching the first row so that each loop becomes a circle. Turn the base upright again. Drop a second line of loops in pairs from the centre of the first loops, leaving one loop out, and then drop a third line of single loops, also from the centre of the pairs of loops. Pipe a snailstrail around the bottom edge.

Assembling the figures

Use a bag with a No2 size hole and thick royal icing. For the bride pipe a line down the straight edge of one of the skirt pieces. Attach to the main body, as shown, with the body still flat on the wax paper. Prop in position with foam rubber and leave to dry. When dry, put thick royal icing on the underside of the body and skirt. Stand upright and attach to the base.

Pipe a line down the straight edge and underside of another skirt piece and attach to the body opposite the first piece. Continue in the same way with the remaining four pieces of the skirt.

For the groom, remove all pieces from the wax paper, but leave the centre piece of groom lying flat on the wax paper. Pipe a line of icing down the straight line of the trousers. Attach this to the main part of the body. When dry, pipe a line of thick royal icing under the trousers and the body and attach it to the base. Hold by the trousers to stand it up, and prop in position. Put thick royal icing on the other section of the trousers down the straight edge and underneath, and fix it to the main body.

Sugarpaste

Smooth-as-silk sugarpaste makes a beautiful beginning for a celebration cake. Such finishing touches as crimper work and ribbon insertion can be used on a sugarpasted cake, while techniques such as embroidery and extension work can look equally good on royal icing or sugarpaste. The sugarpasted bell-shaped wedding cake shown here has been decorated with lace, ribbons and sugar flowers.

Working with Sugarpaste

Sugarpaste is a good medium for a beginner to use for covering a cake, as a good finish can be achieved without too much difficulty. However, a really smooth, glossy finish with evenly rounded edges does take some practice. Most cake decorators use commercial, rather than homemade, sugarpaste.

Marzipanning the cake

Because a sugarpasted cake has rounded edges, the marzipan undercoat should also have rounded edges. To apply the marzipan coating, place the cake on a clean, dry work surface. It is important that the surface be free of flour or cornflour, as these can become trapped between the layers of marzipan and sugarpaste and cause fermentation.

Be sure that the cake is level, and cut off the top if it has formed a dome during baking. Brush the surface of the cake with warm, slightly thinned apricot jam purée.

On a clean, dry surface, lightly knead the marzipan. Sprinkle the surface with a little sifted icing sugar, and roll out the marzipan to the approximate shape of the cake. Check the exact size with a piece of string. Position the cake on the sugared surface.

Use the marzipan spacers to ensure that it is the same thickness all over, then smooth it over until shiny with the sugarpaste smoothers. Lift the sheet of marzipan on a long rolling pin and position it over, but not touching, the cake. Gently lower it over the cake until the cake is completely covered. The edge of the marzipan should just touch the work surface.

Remove the rolling pin and gently smooth the marzipan over the cake, working from the centre of the top up the sides. Put in the corners if the cake has them. Do not pull down on the marzipan, which could make it tear on the upper edge. Instead, pull the marzipan away from the cake and gently pull up to make the corner.

Use both hands to smooth the marzipan and firmly stick it to the cake. Then take a marzipan smoother in each hand and smooth over the surface to eliminate any dents or bumps. Smooth around all corners and along the upper edge, creating round, smooth edges. Cut away any excess marzipan. Fill in any gaps or tears with small sausages of marzipan and smooth again.

Carefully position the cake on a cake board and place in a cake box. Leave in a cool, dry place for several days before coating with sugarpaste.

Applying the sugarpaste

A cake does not need to be marzipanned before coating with sugarpaste. It can be covered with a single, thick layer of sugarpaste, or with two thin layers, as if the first layer was marzipan. If using two thin layers, apply the first as for marzipan and leave to dry for a few days.

To apply the final sugarpaste layer, position the cake on a clean, dry work surface. Moisten the marzipan with a sponge dipped in colourless spirit, such as white rum or Kirsch. This acts as an antibacterial agent. If no alcohol is available, use a little boiled water.

Knead the sugarpaste on a clean, dry sugar-free surface and knead until smooth and pliable. Place it with pleated side down and roll on a sugared surface to the approximate shape required. Use the spacers to ensure that the paste is an even thickness and check that it is the correct size.

Pick up the paste with a rolling pin and gently lower it across the cake. Remove the rolling pin. Carefully lift the sides of the sugarpaste, brushing the surface in one direction to eliminate any air trapped between the layers. Reposition and put in any corners. Avoid stretching the paste, as there is no way to disguise a torn sugarpaste coating other than by positioning decorations over the tear, which may not be in the right place for the design.

When all the corners are in place, smooth all over the surface with the sugarpaste smoothers. If any air bubbles are present, prick them with a very fine needle inserted at an acute angle. Smooth with your hands, then finish with the smoothers.

Trim around the base of the cake carefully. Prepare a board by placing a small piece of moistened sugarpaste in the centre, then position the cake centrally on the board. Use a ruler to check that it is in the correct place. Use the smoothers to give the coating a final smoothing. Check that the base is tightly fastened down.

Painting on Sugarpaste

Beautiful effects can be created by using edible colouring and artist's brushes to paint directly onto sugarpaste or marzipan.

The coating must be completely dry and hard before painting. Either liquid or paste colours can be used. Choose very fine, good quality paint brushes.

If using liquid colours, place a little of the colour on greaseproof paper, dip the brush into the colour, wipe off any excess onto the paper until no streaks appear, then paint on the cake. Never paint directly from the bottle or the colours will run.

The technique is similar if using paste colours. Put a little water on the greaseproof paper first, then add the colour.

If painting something like the patchwork quilt shown here, use one colour at a time and paint it in squares on the quilt. If painting another colour on top, allow the first colour to dry before painting in the next one.

Father Christmas and Reindeer Cake
For this amusing Christmas cake, start with a 23 x 12cm (9 x 5in) cake and place it on a coloured marzipan carpet on a 30cm (12in) square board. Coat the cake with buttercream and make the bedding from sugarpaste. Allow the headboards to dry before assembling the cake. Place sausages of marzipan in the bed to make the bodies before covering with the quilt. Paint the patch quilt as described here. The figures are marzipan with sugarpaste, royal icing and marzipan trimmings.

51

Ribbon Work

Ribbon work, which includes ribbon banding, bows and ribbon insertion, can be very attractive and can add dramatic colour to a cake.

Ribbon banding

Decide first how many ribbon bands the cake should have. If there is to be a single band, choose 3mm (⅛in) ribbon, but for a series of bands use 15mm (½in) ribbon.

Be sure the cake is level before attaching the ribbon. To ensure that the ribbons go on straight, draw a line around the cake using a pair of dividers. Decide on the height for the ribbon. With one arm of the dividers touching the board and the other gently dragging against the surface of the cake, scratch a line onto the cake. It will then be easy to attach the ribbon in a straight line.

Place the cake on a turntable. Pipe a dot of royal icing onto the cake and attach the ribbon. Hold the ribbon in place with a glass-headed pin. Take the ribbon around the cake, adding dots of royal icing as needed. Finish by piping a dot of icing next to the pin. Cut off the ribbon, leaving enough for a slight crossover, and insert another glass-headed pin. When the icing is dry, carefully remove the pins. Disguise the join with a tiny bow or an appliquéd flower.

To hide an untidy sugarpaste edge, or for a simple decorative effect, position a ribbon band against the cake and just touching the board. Pipe a snailstrail along the join of the ribbon at the board. The snailstrail hides the join in the ribbon. The cake can then be finished with extension work, flounces or other designs.

An unusual use of ribbon banding is to attach the band in the usual way, and then pipe a series of fine lines over the ribbon at regular intervals. This gives the impression that the ribbon has been inserted, but is easier to do than ribbon insertion. You can also pipe embroidery onto a wide ribbon band.

A series of ribbon bands and bows in dramatic colours makes this cream oval sugarpasted cake into a celebration centrepiece.

Bows

If planning to combine bows with ribbon insertion, always tie the bows first. The offcuts can then be used for insertion, rather than wasted.

To make the bow, hold the ribbon in your right hand. Allow a tail of about 12cm (5in). Make a loop the size of three fingers of your left hand, and hold the loop between the thumb and forefinger of your right hand. Take the ribbon down and back behind the loop, crossing the forefinger of your right hand. Drop the loose end in front of your thumb, crossing over it. Grasp and twist the loose end and insert it through the loop. Catch the ribbon and pull it tight. Pull the tail of each ribbon until you have a small, flat, neat bow. Cut the tails to the right length.

Ribbon insertion

Ribbon insertion is nearly always combined with crimper work, so it is very important to plan the design before coating the cake. Crimper work is done while the sugarpaste is still soft, but ribbon insertion is best done when the coating is a day or two old — with a crust but not yet hard.

There are several styles of ribbon insertion. The pieces of ribbon can be the same length as the spaces between, making it look as though a band of ribbon has been threaded through the icing. The ribbon pieces can be smaller than the spaces, and broderie anglaise incorporated in the design.

The ribbons can either be folded over and inserted in the paste, or the ends can be left free to form part of the design. This last technique is known as flicked ribbons.

Choose the width of ribbon and plan where the spaces and insertions will be placed. Mark the spacing very carefully, as the contrasting colour of the ribbon will make any errors in positioning very obvious.

To insert the ribbon, use a very fine-bladed knife to cut slits in the sugarpaste. The slits should only be just wide enough to take the ribbon. Cut the ribbons slightly longer than the spaces between the slits, leaving a bit to tuck in. Tuck the ends in with the knife or with the point of a pin. The ribbon should stay in place without any royal icing.

If using ribbons to accentuate crimper work, cut a single slit for each piece of ribbon. Fold the ribbon in half and insert the cut ends into the slit. Make sure each piece of ribbon is the same distance from the surface of the cake.

When using the flicked ribbon technique, cut all the ribbon pieces to the same length. To judge the size, insert the first piece of ribbon, cut to size and remove it. Cut the rest of the pieces to this size.

To insert the ribbon, make two slits where the ribbon is to go. Insert the ribbon in the left-hand slit, and with the point of the knife, gently gather the ribbon to form a small loop. Insert the ribbon into the second slit until the loop disappears. Cut the ends of the ribbon. Repeat with the rest of the ribbon pieces.

Frills and Flounces

When South African cake decorator Elaine Garrett introduced her Garrett frill a few years ago it was the first 'new' idea in cake decorating for many years. There are also several straight frill cutters available.

It is usual to apply the frills and flounces to cakes that have been coated for a few days so the icing is firm to work on. You can, however, disguise the way the flounce is attached to a freshly coated cake by using crimpers over the join while the coating is still pliable.

The frills and flounces can also be applied to royal-iced cakes. Fasten them to the cake with royal icing; this is a little more fiddly than using water. Tint the paste slightly with a colour used elsewhere on the cake. Sugarpaste is not as white as well made royal icing, so a white frill might look discoloured. Another trick is to use coloured icing for the snailstrail, to break the impact of the different whites, then petal dust the frill to tone in. If you want to use a white frill, coat the cake in a colour.

Basic Garrett frill

Mark the design on the side of the cake, leaving enough room below the design for the frill. Pipe a shell design or snailstrail around the base of the cake, and attach a ribbon band if wished. Roll out a medium-sized piece of sugarpaste until it is translucent, and cut out the frills. Choose the correct-sized centre: the larger the hole the narrower the frill will be. The design determines how the circle of paste is cut. For a large frill, cut once, but for small scallops cut the paste into two before starting. There is then less chance of stretching the paste.

Take a cocktail stick and firmly press it into the first segment of the scallop. Each segment should have about 10-12 lines marked. After a few lines stop and gently lift the paste to encourage the frill. When the whole section is complete, paint a little water onto the side of the cake, fractionally below the design line. Fold over the left-hand edge of the frill and stick it to the cake in the appropriate place. Carefully tuck in the right-hand side before fastening that to the cake. Repeat this process all around the cake. The two turned-back edges at the upper point of each scallop should touch, but not overlap.

Finish off the upper edge of the frill with a pattern tracing wheel. Pipe in stitching if wished. A line of embroidery immediately above the frill finishes it off. Another way of finishing is a fine line of snailstrail piped onto the surface of the cake

A single frill looks elegant on this heart-shaped wedding cake (below). The Christening Cake (right) uses layers of petal-dusted scalloped flounces to create a delicate feminine look. The unusual upsidedown flounce (page 53) looks good when combined with colourful inserted ribbons.

immediately above the frill. A band of lace can be attached to the cake just above the frill.

Straight flounce

Flounces are made by the same basic technique as frills. Design the cake. Mark the design onto the side of the cake, positioning it high enough so that the flounce does not touch the board. Finish off the base of the cake.

Roll out a piece of sugarpaste on icing sugar until it is translucent. Cut out the circles with the Garrett frill cutter. Cut the holes to the correct size. Cut through the frill at one side. Partially straighten the flounce. Starting at one end, roll a cocktail stick quickly and firmly along each individual segment of the flounce, encouraging it to frill where necessary. Fold over 5mm (¼in) on either end of the frill. Paint water onto the side of the cake just below the guideline and stick the frill to the cake, making sure that it is straight. Repeat this process all around the cake, carefully overlapping all the joins. Use a cocktail stick to disguise the fact that you have joins.

This type of frill looks most attractive when done in two or three layers, with each layer a paler tone of the layer below. Always apply the layers from the bottom up. It looks particularly attractive when it is then topped off with a band of ribbon gently fixed over the frill where it is attached to the cake. A little petal dust can also give a delightful effect.

Flounce (straight with scalloped upper edge)

This type of flounce is usually applied in two or three layers. Apply the lowest layer as described above, after you have finished off the base of the cake.

Roll out the sugarpaste until translucent, as usual. Cut out the pieces with the Garrett frill cutter and then the holes. Cut each frill in half. Frill the edge of the half frills as described. Fold in 5mm (¼in) on either side of the frill. Place on the palm of your left hand and paint a little water onto the top edge at the back, over the folds. Attach to the cake. Repeat this process all around the cake, carefully overlapping the left-hand edge of the one already in place. Make sure the points are neatly over one another. When you come to the last scallop gently lift

the first scallop attached and tuck the last one underneath the first scallop, thus completing the circle. Finish off with a pattern marker to give the appearance of stitches, a piped snailstrail, embroidery, or a combination of the three.

Scalloped flounce (join disguised with crimping)

In this technique, one, two or three layers of frill are put onto the cake in scallops. Where the scallops join, the surface of the cake below the frill is visible. Position embroidery here to link with the embroidery above the scallop.

Mark the design onto the cake. Roll out the paste, cut it out and flounce as before. Fold in the left-hand side of the flounce 5mm (¼in). Attach it to the cake after painting water onto the cake below the design line. Repeat the process, overlapping the folded end of the flounce over the edge already on the cake. Tuck a finger beneath that section where they join and lift the flounce slightly. This lifts the flounce away from the side of the cake. Repeat this process all around the cake, lifting each joined section.

Subsequent layers are added above in the same way.

This makes a very full, skirted decoration on the cake. Take a crimper and gently crimp the edge of the flounce where it joins the cake, keeping most of the crimping on the cake and not on the flounce. If you cut through the flounce it will fall off the cake.

Attach a tiny bow at each point of the scallop. Complete the decoration with embroidery both above and below the flounce.

Upsidedown flounce

This gives a very busy look to a cake and should be used with something very simple.

Place a thin piece of foam on the surface of the cake, place a piece of perspex over it, then very quickly invert the cake onto a turntable covered with a slightly damp cloth. Attach the layers of frill as for the scalloped flounce. There will be a semicircle at the base of each frill between it and the board. Leave the cake upsidedown for 30 minutes, then carefully turn it right-side up. Insert ribbons or pipe embroidery in the semicircles.

Embossing

This is a very attractive, simple way of decorating a cake. It is also an excellent way of disguising a cake with a poor surface, such as sugarpaste with bubbles or visible hairline cracks showing. It can also be used to great advantage with embroidery, appliqué and flounces.

Embossing must be done when the sugarpaste covering has just been applied. Take a plastic doily and place it with the right side to the cake, centering the main design. With an assistant holding the doily, firmly roll a rolling pin across the cake. Place the rolling pin on one side of the cake and, with a single move, roll right across the cake and off the other side. Do not hesitate or there will be an indentation mark from the rolling pin. A complete imprint of the doily will result.

If wished, decorate the individual flowers in the design with paste colours or petal dust. A light dusting of petal dust can be very effective. Finish off the sides of the cake using the frill and crimper work.

There are many leather embossing tools available from craft shops which can be used on cakes, on the edges of plaques, on cards and on sugar flowers. Again, all the work must be done while the paste is soft. Embossing tools can texture the 'material' on a dress in a piece of bas-relief, fix an attractive centre into a flower, or simply add another dimension to the work. Try out the designs off the cake first.

Crimper Work

Easter Egg Cake
Place the egg-shaped cake off-centre on a 23cm (9in) board and coat with pale green sugarpaste. Emboss both cake and board with a plastic doily. Apply frills and finish with crimper work. The spray of sweet peas is seasonal and attractive.

Crimper tools, sometimes called nippers, come in a combination of different shapes and widths. The most commonly used ones are 10mm (3/8in) wide and come in nine shapes: straight, curve, oval, vee, diamond, scallop, double scallop, heart and holly.

The shapes can be used on their own or combined to make a great number of different patterns. Crimper work can also be used attractively with other techniques, such as embroidery, lace, ribbon work, with embossing, appliqué, over-piping, or for disguising the join of the flounce to the cake.

Practice the design on a piece of sugarpaste before coating the cake.

Crimper work must be done on freshly applied sugarpaste. The crimpers must be clean and dry. Dust them with a little cornflour to prevent sticking. Adjust the crimpers to the right aperture, which depends on the size of the design, and hold with an elastic band. The wider the aperture, the more ridged effect will result when the crimpers are closed. Adjust the apperture by sliding the elastic band higher or lower along the crimper.

To make a crimper design, insert the crimpers into the sugarpaste, pinch together, release and move. If you forget to release the crimpers, a section of the paste will be torn.

If combining crimper work with ribbon banding, use a pair of dividers to mark both the line where the ribbon will be fastened and the lines where the crimper work will go. Complete the crimper work before adding the ribbon and the embroidery.

Embroidery between the two bands of curves gives a very dainty effect. A slight variation is the use of embroidery and embossing in alternate ovals. Combinations of appliqué and embroidery can also give a variety of effects.

On wedding or engagement cakes, very pretty designs can be created with the heart-shaped crimpers. The designs can be emphasised with embroidery or embossing. Butterflies can be created by using the heart-shaped crimpers in pairs, with a body piped between.

If there is a scalloped design on the side of a cake which will be decorated with lace, it makes an attractive change to mark out the scallops using a variety of crimpers. Once the coating has set, apply the lace as usual.

The Garrett frill or the flounce is usually attached when the coating has set. The join then has to be finished off with embroidery, snailstrail or stitching, but it will always be obvious how the frill or flounce was done. If, however, the flounce or frill is attached to the cake while the icing is still fresh, it is possible to completely disguise how it was attached by using crimper work on the join. Be careful not to cut through the frill. Most of the crimping is done on the cake rather than on the frill.

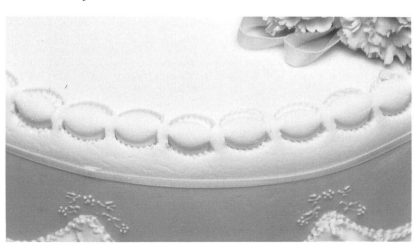

Bas-Relief and Appliqué

These are methods for producing two-dimensional decorations, either on the top or around the sides of a cake. It can be very quick to do if there is little time, or painstaking and slow, depending on how much time is available.

Bas-relief

Work directly onto the surface of the cake, or on a sugarpaste plaque, prepared ahead of time.

Bas-relief is normally done with sugarpaste, but if producing a more complex clothed figure, then it is advisable to use flower paste for the clothing, which gives a more delicate result with the more pliable paste. Bas-relief involves painting, which many cake decorators enjoy.

First select a design. Trace the design onto a piece of tracing paper. Turn it over and repeat the tracing on the other side. Do not transfer graphite onto a cake. A finely sharpened brown lip-pencil on the underside of the tracing can be used. Apply this lightly, as it can smudge easily. Position the design correctly before starting to paint in the background.

Painting can be done either with paste colours, liquid colours or petal dust, or a combination of all three. Put in the delicate, pale colours first, gradually working up to the detail. Most details can be inserted once the figure is in place. Do not use too much liquid. Dip the brush in the colour, then wipe it gently on a white tissue before touching the cake or plaque.

Now roll out a piece of sugarpaste about 5mm (¼in) thick. Trace around the outline of the figure. Remove the tracing paper and cut around the figure with a very sharp knife or a modelling knife. Moisten the underside of the figure and place it on the cake, fitting it into the design. Don't fasten it down too well, or it may be difficult to add pieces of paste to the design before decoration. With a fingertip, gently round off all the cut edges so the pieces do not look cut out.

Using a dresden tool, depress the areas of the figure which need to be in the background (the back leg if one leg is in front of the other, etc.). To accentuate an area and make it more rounded, gently lift the edge of the figure and insert a small ball of paste in the required place. If you want to give the impression that clothing is being worn you can use the flat tip of the dresden tool to slice the figure on the junction and gently lift up the piece of clothing, smoothing the cut surface below. If the tip of the dresden tool is not fine enough the point of a modelling knife can be used. Make sure that the surface is smooth and rounded where needed and create as many creases and folds as are needed elsewhere.

Once the modelling has been completed, a little piped royal icing can be used to complete the design. Paint in any decoration required with paste colours or use petal dust. Use the petal dust sparingly or it will spread onto areas where it is not wanted and spoil the picture.

If making clothed figures the process is a little different. Start the same way, tracing the basic design onto tracing paper, and transfer the design to the cake as before. Paint in the background. Roll out the sugarpaste 5mm (¼in) thick. Cut out a basic figure, without clothes or clothed limbs. A bare limb can be cut out now. Once again, moisten the underside of the figure and attach it to the cake.

Roll out flower paste in the colour chosen and cut the items of clothing. Attach them to the figure. When making a figure in a dress, put the skirt on first, bending the sides so that it looks as if it goes all around the figure. Add the bodice, then the collar, then the apron, and attach the pocket. Cut the sleeves and attach them to arms. Work the hands carefully and then attach the arms covered with sleeves to the rest of the figure. It is very easy to pleat the flower paste to make it look as though it is gathered, frilled, etc.

Paint in any detail you require. If the figure is wearing a sweater, you can create the illusion of knitwear using a very fine tube and royal icing. Hair can be piped on later. Paint in any features and highlight the clothing. Additional features such as grass, tiny baskets, and flowers are added last.

Appliqué

This technique can be used on cakes or on pastillage cards. If the work is to be done directly onto the cake it is better to use sugarpaste rather than flower paste.

Designs such as wine bottles, glasses and beer mugs can be cut from paste and stuck to the sides or the top of the cake. They can then be embellished with royal icing. Flower designs are also popular. Combine a series of embroidered stems and create three-dimensional effect with appliquéd petals and flowers.

You will need a collection of small, simple cutters, a pad of foam rubber, ball tools, crank-handled palette knife, modelling knife, tulle, royal icing with No0 and 1 tubes.

Make a template of the design. Transfer it onto the surface of the cake. Paint in the background, pipe on stems, etc, and then roll out the sugarpaste very thinly. Cut out the flowers. If you wish to make them look more lifelike, place them on a pad of foam rubber and press the petals and flowers into shape with ball tools. If making daisies, impress the straight lines onto each petal, cup the centre of the flower, make the centre using tulle and then stick the flower onto the stem piped on the side of the cake.

Pixie Birthday Cake

This adorable pixie cake would enhance any little girl's birthday party. It combines a variety of cake-decorating techniques to great effect. Coat a 15cm (6in) round cake with white sugarpaste. Decorate the sides with upsidedown frills, ribbon insertion and embroidery. The three-dimensional pixie is made from bas-relief and appliqué sugarpaste and flower paste.

Broderie Anglaise

Broderie anglaise, sometimes called eyelet embroidery, is similar to other tube embroidery techniques. Copy designs from embroidery pattern transfers or from a piece of cotton broderie anglaise, and lightly mark it onto sugarpaste which has been allowed to skin. Use a fine knitting needle to mark the holes in the design. Using medium-peak royal icing and a No 0 or 00 piping tube, pipe around the hole and then circle the rim carefully to finish off. Pipe the rest of the design using the same tube. Broderie anglaise is most attractive when piped in pale colours or in white. Work carefully, as mistakes tend to be very obvious.

Embroidered collars

Broderie anglaise can look lovely on a sugarpaste collar, as on this charming christening cake. To make the collars, trace the top and bottom templates and cut out with scissors. Roll out the sugarpaste to the size of the board. Smooth with a smoother, and pin the templates in place, positioning the pins where the embroidery will go. Cut round the templates with a sharp knife. Crimp the edges, remove the templates, and leave the sugarpaste to harden for a day or two.

When the sugarpaste has skinned, mark the indentations for the broderie anglaise. Pipe the outlines with a No 00 tube. Leave the collars to dry for about a week before assembling the cake.

The christening cake shown here is an 18cm (7in) round cake, positioned on a 33cm (13in) board. Royal ice the sides of the cake, and make the embroidered collars from the templates shown here. Attach the collars with a small amount of royal icing.

If wished, place a crib made from sugarpaste in the centre of the cake, or top with one of the modelled babies shown on page 78.

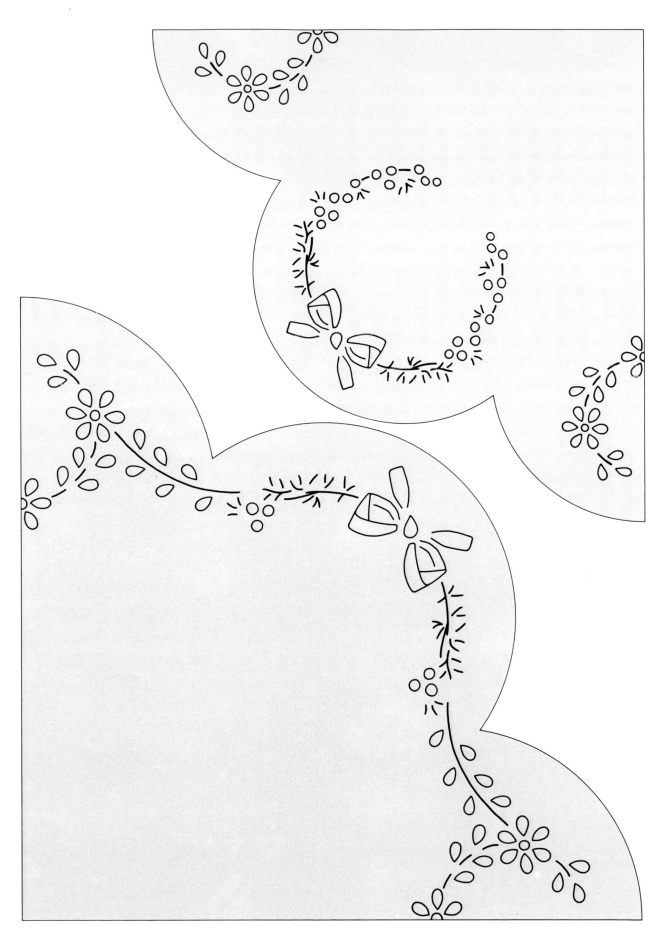

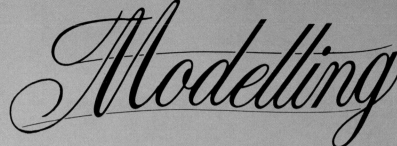

Modelling

One of the most charming skills of the cake decorator is modelling figures from marzipan and modelling paste. Marzipan is most often used, and the results which can be achieved are shown in the Frog Band Cake on this page. It is possible to produce every animal in the zoo from marzipan, as well as more 'human' figures such as fairies, and the figures can be arranged on cakes or left as free-standing ornaments. All that is needed is an understanding of the basic techniques and a little imagination.

Working with Marzipan

Marzipan is a paste which is usually made from ground almonds and sugar. It is most often used to cover cakes before they are iced, but it can also be coloured and used as the only coating on rich fruit cakes, rather than as an undercoat. Modelled figures made from marzipan are attractive decorations for celebration cakes for all occasions.

Whether coating a cake or modelling, the same basic rules apply to all work with marzipan. First, make sure that the work surfaces and tools are clean and free from any dirt or grease. Thoroughly wash hands and clean fingernails before beginning work. Most work surfaces should be sprinkled with icing sugar, never with flour or cornflour, which can cause the marzipan to ferment. However, if using a non-stick surface, such as a special plastic board, it is not necessary to use icing sugar. The paste should be worked very carefully to ensure that there are no cracks, which can allow air in and lead to fermentation.

When colouring marzipan for modelling, use edible paste colours, as liquid ones will tend to change the texture of the paste. To colour marzipan, cut off the amount necessary to make the figure, put a small amount of colouring paste in the middle and knead until the colour is evenly distributed. Start with a very small amount of colour. If the marzipan is too light then add more colour; if too dark, add a little more marzipan.

Marzipan figures should be left to dry in the open air for about 24 hours. When dry, a small amount of liquid food colouring can be painted on with a fine brush to add details. Never store finished articles in an airtight container, or the figures may become limp or sticky. Keep them in a cardboard cake box or something similar.

Making marzipan

Most cake decorators prefer to use commercially made marzipan, which is available in packets from large supermarkets and specialist shops. For best results, buy white marzipan rather than the yellow almond paste. The figures shown on the following pages can be made from this cooked almond paste, but homemade paste tends to be sticky and more difficult to work with than commercial marzipan.

Boiled Almond Paste
Makes about 350g (12oz)

200g (7oz/1¾ cups) sugar

120ml (4fl oz/½ cup) water

pinch cream of tartar

150g (5oz/1¼ cups) ground almonds

1-2 drops almond essence or extract

1 large egg white

icing (confectioner's) sugar, for dusting

Put the sugar and water into a small saucepan and cook over low heat, stirring occasionally, until the sugar is dissolved. Add the cream of tartar and quickly bring to the boil. Boil until it reaches a temperature of 116°C (240°F), or soft ball stage. Remove from the heat and beat until the mixture turns cloudy. Add the ground almonds and almond essence or extract. Whisk the egg white lightly and add to the pan. Return to low heat and cook for 2 minutes, stirring constantly. Turn out the paste onto a board lightly dusted with icing sugar, cover with cling film and leave until cold. Knead until smooth and free of cracks. Wrap in a plastic bag and store in a cool, dry place if not needed immediately.

Making Marzipan Figures

When modelling figures in marzipan, try to make each figure an individual character with its own story to tell. All figures are based on the same three basic shapes – the ball, the sausage and the cone. The step-by-step photographs here show how to make a marzipan teddy bear, and all of the figures on the following pages are made in a similar way. Most modelled figures require between 30g (1oz) and 100g (4oz) of marzipan, and the amounts given in all of the instructions are just a guideline. For larger or smaller figures, be sure to keep the same proportions.

Equipment
For a 5cm (2in) high teddy bear, you will need about 60g (2oz) marzipan. Assemble the coloured marzipan, a small, sharp knife, a ball tool, piping bag (No2) with white royal icing, piping bag (No1) with dark brown royal icing.

1 To make the body, cut off 30g (1oz) marzipan and roll into a ball. Rock the ball between the heels, not the palms, of your hands to make a cone, and flatten the top of the cone slightly.

2 For the head, cut off 10g (⅓oz) marzipan and roll in the palms of your hands to make a cone. Make indentations for the eye sockets with a ball tool. Press in firmly and then move the handle upwards. Cut the mouth sideways with a sharp knife, then press down gently to open. Squeeze the sides of the mouth to make a smile.

3 For the ears, make two tiny balls and attach firmly to the top of the head. Use a ball tool to make the indentations, supporting the ear with your finger behind it. Make an oval nose with a bit of brown marzipan and attach in position.

4 Fill the eye sockets with white royal icing. Pipe the pupils with dark brown royal icing, positioning them off centre to give the teddy an expression. If wished, when dry, paint on eyelashes with edible colouring and a fine paint brush.

5 To make the legs, cut 10g (⅓oz) marzipan and roll into a sausage. Indent the outside by rolling it with your little finger to make feet. Cut the sausage in half lengthwise, pinch up feet and mark claws with the back of the knife. Use 7g (¼oz) marzipan for the arms.

6 Assemble the teddy bear. If assembled at the time of making, the pieces should stick together easily. If assembling later, use melted chocolate as glue. Attach the legs, then the arms, and place the head on last. Leave to dry in the open air for 24 hours before storing.

Teddies in Bed Cake
Here is one idea for using modelled
marzipan teddy bears – put them to
bed. The cake itself is 12x20cm
(5x8in). You will also need 900g (2lb)
sugarpaste, 560g (1¼lb) marzipan,
60g (2oz) royal icing and 110g (¼lb)
melted chocolate. The six teddies in
bed are made following the
instructions on this page, while
mother bear is made using four
times the quantities. Put sausages
of marzipan in the bed to represent
the bodies, make a green sausage
for the bolster. Carpet, sheet, quilt,
headboards and mother bear's
dress are sugarpaste. Allow the
headboard to dry for about two
days before assembling. Following
the instructions on page 51, use
edible liquid colours to paint on the
designs. Pieces are attached with
thick royal icing or melted
chocolate. The finishing touches –
slippers, a honey pot for midnight
snacks – are all coloured sugarpaste.

Elephant (90g (3oz) pink paste)
For body and legs, use 50g (1¾oz) to make a fat sausage and cut at both ends for legs. Make indentation with ball tool for toes. Bend to shape. For the head, make a cone shape with 30g (1oz), and elongate the end to make the trunk. Make two round balls for ears and make an indentation with your finger, leaving a ridge around the top edge. Make a small cone for the tail, flatten it and attach in position.

Mouse (40g (1⅓oz) light brown paste/small amount white paste)
Make a cone with 20g (⅓oz) light brown paste. Make an indentation in stomach. Make a smaller cone in white paste, place in indentation and roll until a single smooth cone. Light brown cone for head; gently stroke top to make hair. Cut with scissors. Flatten balls for ears and attach to sides of head. Make indentations with finger and attach to head. Make sausage for arms as for teddy bear. Tail is a long, thin sausage. Feet are small balls of dark brown marzipan.

Dog (50g (1¾oz) dark brown paste) Make a cone for the body with 30g (1oz). Flatten top slightly. Make a fat sausage for the head and with your index finger rock the end from side to side to obtain shape. Small flattened cones for ears, then press pointed end against sides of head. Make small flattened cones for feet, attach, and make indentations for toes. Arms are small sausages. Flatten ends and make indentations Pipe eyes and make a small white nose. Attach a tail.

Cat (50g (1¾oz) white paste) Make a cone for the body with 25g (¾oz) and lay flat. Make a ball for the head and gently pinch up ears. Place your finger behind the ear and press a cocktail stick in the centre to shape the inside. With thumb and forefinger, gently stroke sides of face, then snip with scissors for whiskers. Make indentations for eyes. Pipe eyes and add marzipan nose and mouth. Attach a long sausage for tail.

Kangaroo and baby
(40g (1⅓oz) light brown paste)
For the mother's body, take 20g (⅔oz) marzipan and make a cone. Continue rolling between the palms of your hands to make the tail, the cone top end slightly to form the neck. Flatten top to take head. For the head, make a cone and mark indentations for eyes. Pipe eyes and pupils. Cut mouth. For ears, make a cone, shape indent with ball tool. Make small dark brown ball for nose. For the legs, make a cone and make an indentation for the muscle. Cut down the centre. Flatten ends and mark feet. Bend to shape. Make small cone for arms and make two indentations. Cut down centre. Flatten ends and mark hands. Bend to shape. For the baby, use a small amount of paste to make head and paws as for mother. Add hat and apron if wished.

Koala bear (60g (2oz) brown paste/small amounts white and black paste)
Make a cone for the body with 30g (1oz) brown paste and roll in a white inset as for the Mouse. Flatten top slightly. Make a ball for the head. Gently squeeze and stroke sides, then snip with scissors to represent fur. Brown balls for ears with white insets. Flatten and attach to head. Make indentation with ball tool. Squeeze outside edge of ears and snip with scissors to represent fur. Eyes are black marzipan balls. Nose is a small cone pinched in the middle. Sausages for arms and legs as for teddy bear.

Large chick
(30g (1oz) yellow paste)
Make a cone for the body with 20g (⅔oz) and flatten top. Flatten end for tail and cut with scissors. Cut wings with scissors. Head is a ball. Stroke gently to make feathers on top. Cut with scissors. Make indentations for eyes. Pipe eyes in usual way. Make a small red cone for beak, flatten it and cut the rounded edge with scissors. Make smaller chick in proportion.

69

Monkey (50g (1¾oz) brown paste/10g (⅓oz) pink paste/7g (¼oz) white paste)

For the body, make a cone with 30g (1oz) brown paste and make an indentation in stomach. Make another cone with pink paste and press into stomach. Roll to form a single cone. Make indentation for navel. Arms and legs are long, thin sausages wrapped around body. Flatten ends and cut for feet and hands. Support arms with foam rubber until set. Make a brown cone for the head, indent and place white cone for base of head. Roll to form a single cone. Nose and mouth are tiny pink balls. Ears are white balls, flattened and then attached to sides of head. Indent and pipe eyes.

Lion (60g (2oz) brown paste/small amount of darker brown paste)

Make a cone for the body with 40g (1⅓oz). Cut sides for legs. Position small cones for feet and flatten ends. Mark toes. Make a long sausage and wrap around body for arms. Mark paws. Tail is a sausage. The brush is a flattened dark brown cone snipped with scissors and attached to the end. Make a ball and flatten on work surface to make the head. Use a ball tool to make indentations for features. Mane is a long, thin, dark brown or yellow sausage. Position around head and snip with scissors to make fur. Mouth is a dark brown ball. Indent with a ball tool. Make a dark brown sausage for the moustache, indent in the middle with your little finger and press on the face. Nose is a dark brown ball. Indent with a cocktail stick for nostrils. Leave face to harden before attaching to body. Pipe eyes as for teddy bear.

Rabbit (20g (¾oz) white paste/ 40g (1⅓oz) orange paste)
Make a white cone for the head. Make an indentation with the outside of your little finger for the base of the ears. Cut through to make two ears. Make indentation with ball tool for inside of ears.

Stroke the sides of the head and then snip with scissors for whiskers. Nose is small pink ball. Pipe eyes in usual way. Top of body is orange cone. Arms are orange sausages. Taper the ends. Make holes in the wider ends for paws. Attach small white cones for paws. Make a fat orange sausage for legs, cut as shown and leave on a dusted board to dry overnight. Attach to body and add white feet.

Tortoise (10g (⅓oz) light brown paste/15g (½oz) orange paste)
With light brown paste, make a long sausage for the body and taper at the end for tail. Make indentations for the eyes and cut the mouth. Open mouth and press sides to make smile. Mark nostrils with a cocktail stick and pipe eyes. For the arms, make a long sausage and flatten both ends. Mark hands and place on top of body. Make legs the same way and place at tail end of body. For the shell, make an orange ball and press out the edges between fingers and thumbs. Mark circles with a piping tube and mark edges with a knife. Place shell on top of body.

Duck (30g (1oz) white paste)
Make body and head exactly as for large chick. Pipe eyes. Beak is orange marzipan. Make two small balls for feet, flatten and cut out webbed toes. Add hats, scarves, clothes from coloured marzipan or sugarpaste, if wished.

Basic frog (90g (3oz) green paste)
For the body, make a cone with 50g
(1¾oz) and flatten the top slightly
to take the head. Make a fat cone for
the head and flatten the pointed end
to form the mouth. Cut mouth with
a sharp knife and then place point
inside mouth and press down to
open it. Squeeze sides gently to
make him smile. With finger and
thumb, gently press and stroke the
top of the head to form eyebrows.
Make indentations with a ball tool
for the eye sockets.

  Pipe eyes as for teddy bear. Make
a cone of red marzipan for tongue,
flatten and position in mouth.
Make indentations for nostrils with
a cocktail stick.

  For the legs, make a sausage and
make two indentations on the outside with your little finger. Cut
lengthwise and flatten foot. Cut out
toes. Attach legs to body. Make a
smaller sausage for arms and make
as for legs.

Frog Band Cake

Position a 25cm (10in) round cake to
one edge of a 36cm (14in) cake board
and coat them both with blue sugarpaste. Cut a water lily leaf from
green flower paste and mark veins
with a knitting needle. When dry,
attach to the cake with royal icing.
Reeds and bullrushes are made
from rice paper. Small fish are
coloured marzipan.

  Make the frogs following the
basic instructions on this page.
Clothes and instruments are made
from rice paper, marzipan and
sugarpaste. Position the frogs on
the cake or around it.

Frog Raft Cake

Set frogs to sail on a cake made from six chocolate Swiss rolls coated in brown sugarpaste and placed on a 30cm (12in) square board. Mast is rice paper maché and clothes are coloured rice paper (see page 87). Pipe the rope with pale yellow royal icing and a No 43 tube. Make as many frogs as required and add clothing, hats, pipe, fishing rod, etc made from rice paper maché.

Large Cake-top Decorations

These figures would provide wonderful finishing touches for birthday, christening or engagement cakes. They also make unusual table decorations, party favours or place cards.

Marzipan mouse sleeping in a flower paste leaf. Outside leaf is made from rice paper. Use real leaves for templates.

Marzipan mouse sleeping in a flower paste sardine tin, covered with a painted sugarpaste patch-work quilt.

Marzipan mice in a matchbox. Take apart a real matchbox and trace for a template to make it in rice paper.

Marzipan mice in a rice paper envelope. Take apart a real envelope and trace for a template.

Flower paste cradle made with petal cutters. Cut out the ends with different-sized petal cutters and cut a rectangle of paste in the correct size. Make the holes with a small cutter. Shape the rectangle over a dowel and leave to dry. When all pieces are dry, assemble with thick royal icing. The toys are marzipan and modelling paste.

Marzipan baby in a sugarpaste cradle.

75

Cutouts

Both marzipan and sugarpaste can be used to make flat cake-top decorations. Colour the paste in the usual way, then roll it out on a nonstick surface using a small, nonstick rolling pin. If rolling on a wooden board, dust it with a little icing sugar first.

Decorations can be cut out either with biscuit or aspic cutters, or by using a sharp knife to cut around a greaseproof paper template. To remove from the board, slip a palette knife under the design and carefully lift it off. Position it on the cake, using a bit of royal icing to hold it firmly if necessary.

Christmas Candle Cake
Cover a 25cm (10in) long oval cake with royal icing. Pipe a shell border around the base and attach a ribbon above it. Roll out enough green marzipan to cut 40 holly leaves, and dry over a piece of dowelling dusted with icing sugar. Cut the candle from red marzipan and the flame from yellow, as in the photograph (bottom, right). Make red marzipan berries. Attach the marzipan cutouts to the cake as shown in the photograph.

Santa Claus
This would look good on a 20cm (8in) round cake. Roll out red marzipan or sugarpaste and cut a 10cm (4in) triangle with three equal sides. Assemble the features as shown in the photograph. Position in the centre of the cake when dry.

Christmas tree
Use the photograph to make a template from greaseproof paper. Roll out green marzipan and use a sharp knife to cut round the template. Mark the garlands as shown and pipe in with royal icing and a No1 tube. Push coloured dragees in the soft paste. When dry, attach to a small round or oval cake.

Christmas stocking
Use the photograph to make a template from greaseproof paper. Cut out from red marzipan or sugarpaste. Use white sugarpaste for trimmings. Make the parcels from small pieces of paste and decorate with piped royal icing.

Making Figures from Modelling Paste

Although most of the animals and figures in this chapter are made from marzipan, it is also possible to model figures from modelling paste or flower paste. This is used most often for more delicate figures, such as the fairies shown here, as it sets very hard, keeping a good shape.

Modelling paste is pure white and easy to tint. Use paste or liquid colours and knead into a small piece of paste. If using liquid colours, be sure not to use too much, or the texture of the paste will change. Use gum arabic glue or a little royal icing to assemble the figures.

Choir girl (30g (1oz) red paste/ 10g (⅓oz) skintone paste)

Make a red cone for the body. Use skintone paste to make a ball for the head and place on a cocktail stick. Paint features and hair with black edible colour. Arms are a red sausage tapered at both ends and cut in half. Make a hole in the wide-end for hands, and position two tiny, skintone balls.

Assemble choir girl and decorate with piped white royal icing. Add hats, collars, etc from coloured marzipan or sugarpaste. Books are made from rice paper. See page 83 for Choir Girls Christmas Cake.

Modelling paste fairy
(10g (⅓oz) skintone paste)

Make a cone for the body and elongate it to taper for the legs. Indent three times, cut lengthways and bend legs to required position. Make a hole in the top of the body with a cocktail stick and leave to dry.

Make the clothes from rice paper or modelling paste, and dress the fairy. Arms are thin sausages with flattened hands. Make a ball for the head and use a cocktail stick to make features.

Assemble the fairy, positioning the head and then the rice paper wings (see page 86). Pipe hair with royal icing and dust with petal dust.

See step-by-step of fairy, on the left.

Baby (30g (1oz) pale pink paste)

Make a ball for the head. With your finger, gently indent across the middle and make the eyes with a ball tool. Make a tiny ball for nose. Pipe hair with royal icing. Mark the mouth with a cocktail stick. Ears are tiny question mark shapes. Position on head and leave to set. Paint hair with royal icing; use edible colours for other features.

Make a cone for the body with 15g (½oz) of paste. Arms and legs are tapered sausages. Indent twice with your little finger, cut lengthwise, bend arms and legs into position and attach to body.

Use a cocktail stick to mark line for buttocks on back and make indentation for navel on front. Dust baby with pale pink petal dust when finished. Place on sugarpaste rug if wished.

Toadstool Cake
This cake, which would delight any little girl, uses modelling paste figures. Coat an 18cm (7in) round cake with white royal icing or sugarpaste. Decorate cake and board with leaves cut from modelling paste. For the top decoration, coat a 10cm (4in) thin board with thick green royal icing and stipple to resemble grass. Petals are cut from thinly rolled modelling paste. Flute with a ball tool and petal dust when dry. Toadstools have rice paper stalks and modelling paste caps. Assemble as shown in the photograph, and position a fairy in the centre of the flower.

Rice Paper

Attractive decorations made from rice paper can provide charming finishing touches for a cake. Working with rice paper is one of the easiest decorating techniques — even children can produce pretty decorations with just a little practice. Rice paper can be used to make clothing for marzipan figures, for free-standing figures like the Christmas trees, or as an important feature of a cake, like the fairy castle shown here.

Working with Rice Paper

Rice paper, which is edible, can be purchased from cake decorating shops or large stationers. It is usually A4 size, but can occasionally be bought in rolls. One side of the rice paper is smooth and shiny, while the other side is rough. No special equipment is needed for rice paper work – it can be cut with ordinary scissors or a craft knife and coloured with paste colours and artist's brushes. It can also be coloured with piping jel: buy clear jel and paint on rice paper with a brush. It can then be coloured with either paste or liquid colours. Glue is not necessary for rice paper, as it will stick to itself if moistened slightly. Remember that too much water will make it disintegrate, so use the minimum amount or the objects will lose their shape as they dry. A polystyrene block is useful for drying finished rice paper creations.

Rice paper maché
Decorations can be made from rice paper maché. Simply dampen small pieces of rice paper and use your fingers to mould the desired shape. Place on a polystyrene block to dry — drying times vary according to the size of the object and the humidity. The paper contracts slightly as it dries, so it may be necessary to pin it to the block.

When dry the rice paper maché will be rock hard. It can then be cut with a craft knife or sanded down if required. Use paste colours to paint the finished objects.

Christmas trees
Rice paper can be used to make delightful free-standing Christmas trees. Make tiny ones to decorate the Christmas cake, or larger ones (up to 30cm (12in) high) to use as tabletop decorations.

Cut eight equilateral triangles from rice paper. With the smooth side of the paper on the outside, fold each triangle in half, and snip out small graduated triangles to resemble pine tree branches.

To assemble, dampen the outside of a fold of one triangle with water and press another triangle firmly onto it. Continue in this way until there is a bushy Christmas tree. Dry for about a half hour. Colour with petal dust, piping jel, edible glitter or pens with edible ink.

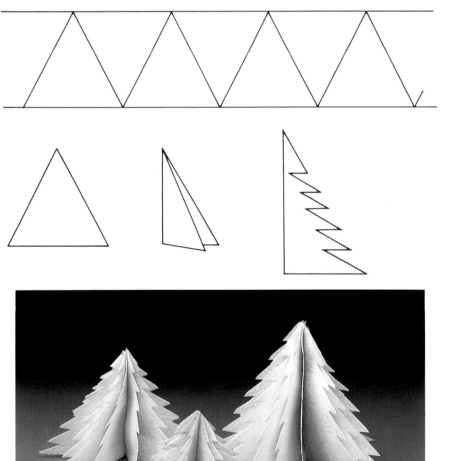

Choir Girls Christmas Cake

Coat an 18cm (7in) round cake with white royal icing. Using a No44 star tube, pipe an even number of stars around the top and bottom edges. With a No1 tube and red royal icing, drop loops from alternate stars, as shown. Pipe lettering if wished.

Assemble lamp and dust with required colour. Position on cake and arrange modelled choir girls around it.

Lantern

Stick the candle into the middle of the modelling paste base and stick the flame on the top. Leave to dry.

Base   **Candle**   **Flame**

Top

Cut from rice paper and cut where marked. Fold to make slight cone, dampen the edge and stick. Leave to dry.

Supports (cut 4)

Stick two pieces of rice paper together with piping jel. Leave to dry and then cut as template and fold over top where indicated.

To assemble

Dampen the folded top of each support and stick to top cone. When dry, fix to base of lamp with thick royal icing. Rice paper can be dusted to colour required.

Fairy Castle Cake

To make the Fairy Castle Cake on page 80, start with a 25cm (10in) cake covered with white royal icing. Make the castle and position on the cake. Stipple stiff royal icing on the sides of the cake with a small palette knife, and petal dust to match the colour scheme when dry. The fairies and clothes are made from modelling paste. The wings are made from rice paper.

Tubes or cylinders

If making a cylinder out of rice paper, always roll the paper with the lengthwise grain. This is always parallel to the longest side of the paper. Cut a strip to the required size and roll the paper with the rough side facing you. Roll it around a pencil or similar object, or omit the pencil for a solid cylinder. Depending on the diameter, roll the paper around at least two or three times. Leave a strip of about 2.5cm (1in) long unrolled. Dip quickly into water, remove any excess moisture with your fingers, then stick this on the cylinder to seal it. Put the finished object on a wooden skewer and press the skewer into a polystyrene block until the cylinder is dry.

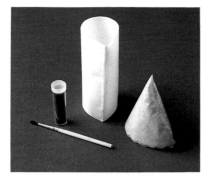

1 For each tower, cut two pieces of rice paper from the roof and tower templates. With the shiny side on the outside, wet one edge and stick together to make a double thickness.

2 Roll each base to make a cylinder, wet edges and stick together. Fold each roof to make a cone and stick together in the same way. Mark scalloped edges using a pen with edible ink. Leave to dry. Colour with petal dust.

3 Assemble the three towers. Dampen the top of each cone and hold the roof in place for a few minutes to make it stick firmly. Draw in windows and door. Make a base of green rice paper maché and stick the towers to it. Position on cake when dry.

Cones and towers for castle

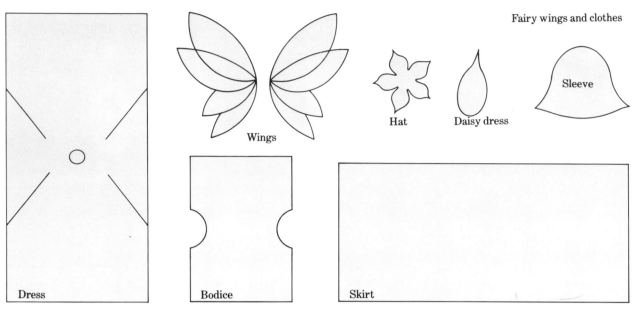

Fairy wings and clothes

Dress

Wings

Hat

Daisy dress

Sleeve

Bodice

Skirt

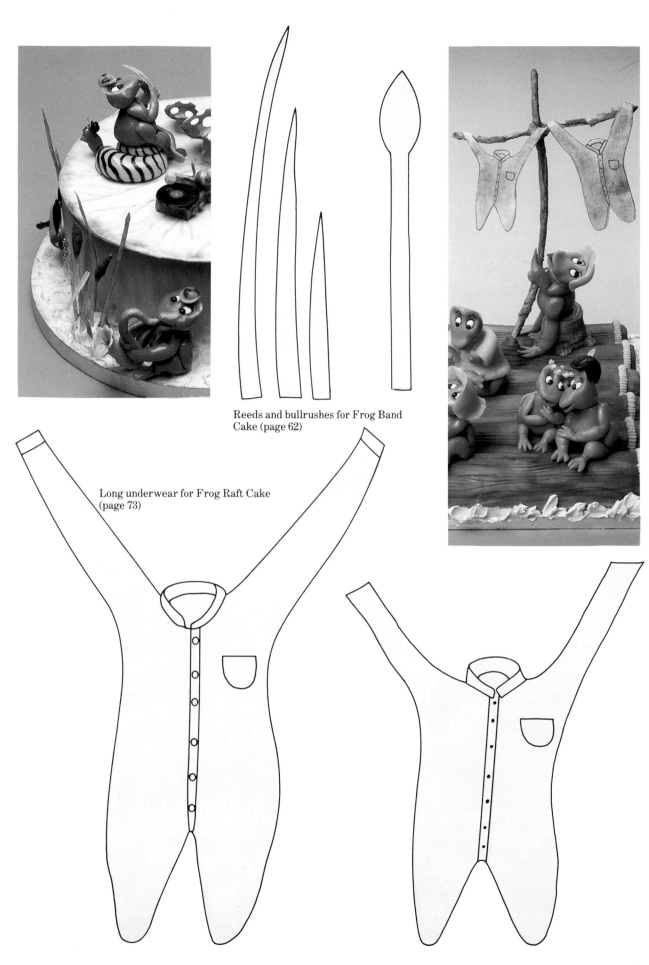

Reeds and bullrushes for Frog Band
Cake (page 62)

Long underwear for Frog Raft Cake
(page 73)

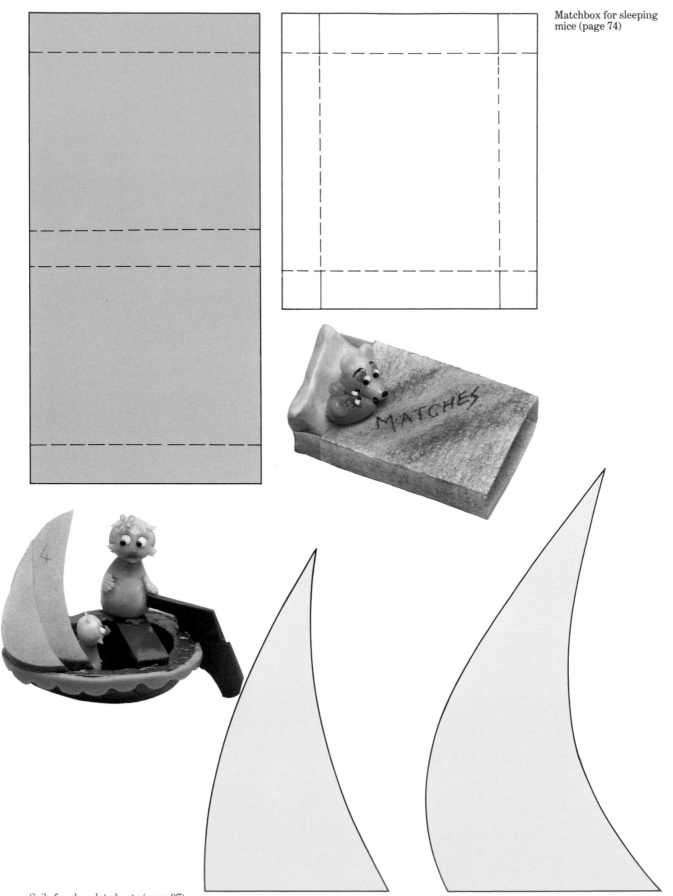

Matchbox for sleeping mice (page 74)

Sails for chocolate boats (page 97)

Envelope for sleeping mice (page 75)

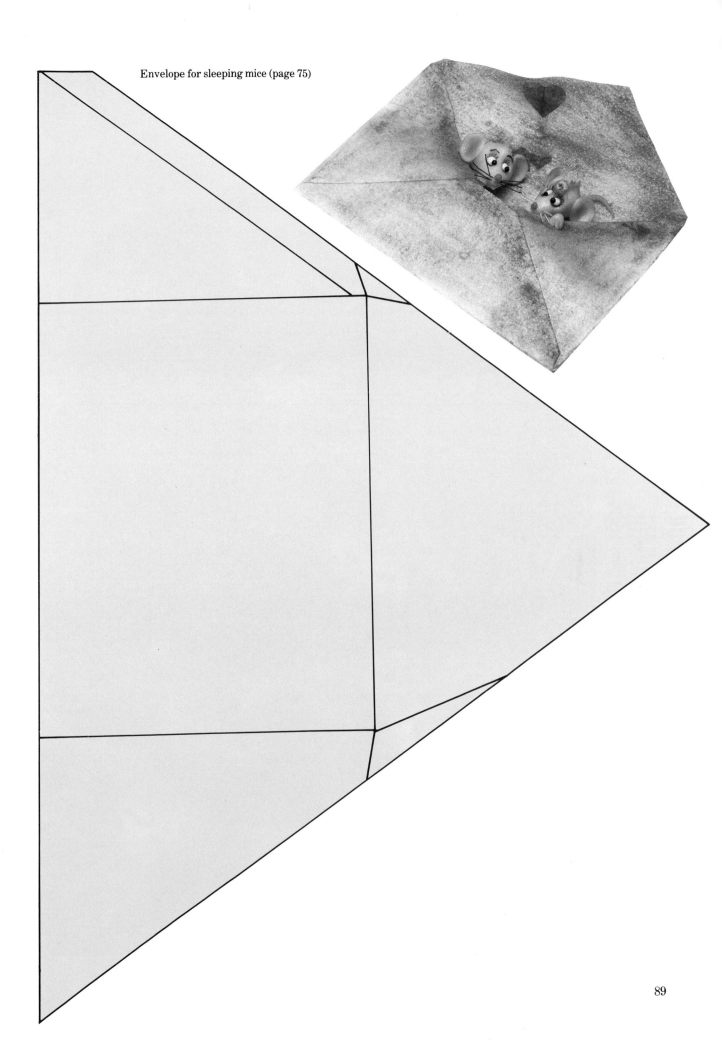

Chocolate

Rich, dark chocolate is a favourite of nearly everyone. A chocolate Easter egg makes a perfect gift, especially a homemade egg. Even a purchased chocolate egg can be made individual and special with a little work. Chocolate can also be used to make pretty decorations for cakes, or even to cover cakes for a unique effect. The exquisite chocolate box shown here is simple to make and would be a welcome gift.

Working with Chocolate

Chocolate work for cake decorations and Easter eggs is most successful when Baker's chocolate is used. This differs from the more expensive chocolate couverture in that most of the cocoa butter has been removed and replaced with hydrogenated fat, and a stabiliser is added to prevent the fat from separating. Baker's chocolate does not need to be tempered, and is therefore quick and convenient to use.

Baker's chocolate is available in dark (plain or semi-sweet), medium and light (milk), and can be purchased in slabs or in small pieces. To melt, place in the top of a double-boiler or in a bowl over a pan of hand-hot water (maximum temperature 38-43°C (100-110°F) and heat until completely melted.

Chocolate leaves

To make chocolate leaves, choose real leaves for moulds, such as those from roses or fuchsias which have well-defined veins. Pick the leaves, leaving a bit of stem to make handling easier. Wash and dry them well.

Melt the chocolate. Using a small paint brush, thickly coat the underside of the leaf with melted chocolate. The coating should be smooth and fairly thick, and should come to the edge of the leaf but not overlap, or removing the leaf will be difficult. Place on wax paper or greaseproof paper and leave in a cool place until set, which could take up to an hour.

When the chocolate is firm, carefully peel off the leaf and place the chocolate leaf on waxed or greaseproof paper. Store in a cool place until needed.

Chocolate cutouts

These can make attractive decorations for a simply iced cake. First, prepare a baking sheet by lining it with greaseproof paper. Melt the chocolate and pour it onto the paper, spreading it evenly with a palette knife. Pick up the greaseproof paper and allow to drop several times so that the chocolate runs level and any air bubbles break. When the chocolate has set, use a sharp knife or cutters to make the desired shapes.

Chocolate cones

A chocolate cone can be used as a cake decoration or as an attractive party favour. The cones can be

filled with marzipan fruit or figures, nuts, or small sweets.

Melt Baker's chocolate in the usual way. Make a small piping bag from greaseproof paper and tape the seam. Insert a small plastic container into the bag and hold the flap against the container with your forefinger. Pour a thick coating of chocolate around the cone. When it is well covered, place it on a board with the flap side down. Leave in the container to hold the shape.

Use a thick paintbrush to stipple some more chocolate on the cone to give a log appearance. Leave in a cool room for several hours, or until the chocolate is firm.

When set, remove the container, and then remove the bag by peeling the edge away from the sides of the cone. Twist the bag between your fingers and gently pull it away from the chocolate.

Chocolate box

To make the chocolate box, choose one of the commercial moulds available. Fill with melted chocolate, following the instructions for Easter eggs, and allow the chocolate to set completely before unmoulding.

Decorate the box with a flower made from flower paste, if wished. Fill with purchased chocolates, or make homemade chocolates using commercially available moulds.

Chocolate Castle Cake

A wonderful castle cake will be the delight of every boy's birthday party. Start with a cake 18cm (7in) square and 7.5cm (3in) high. Coat with buttercream, then top with sugarpaste. Make a template, pour out the melted chocolate onto greaseproof paper, and mark out as shown. Cut out the turrets, then mark the brickwork lightly. When the castle wall has set, gently lift from the greaseproof paper and attach to the cake with melted chocolate. Decorate with small figures if wished.

Easter Eggs

Easter eggs can be decorated in an infinite variety of imaginative ways. Silk or sugar flowers, piped edgings, marzipan decorations are all suitable. The eggs shown in this chapter are just a few ideas for unique Easter gifts.

Easter egg animals

All of these charming figures are based on 'egg-sized' chocolate eggs. Make your own eggs from commercial moulds, or use purchased chocolate eggs. The fondant-filled eggs available at Easter are useful for these animals, as they are solid and heavy enough to support the weight of the marzipan.

Using the chocolate egg as the body, make heads, limbs and tails following the instructions for marzipan figures on page 66. Attach the marzipan with melted chocolate. Make a chocolate base, or position figures on thin cake boards. These eggs make delightful favours for parties.

Making chocolate eggs

There are a number of different Easter egg moulds on the market, all of which give good results.

Polish the moulds with cotton wool or a paper towel, and then pour in the melted chocolate. Chocolate for Easter eggs should be heated to 38-43°C (100-110°F). If the chocolate is too hot, the eggs will have white streaks, and if it is too cool, a white bloom will appear on the surface.

Leave the moulds in a cool place until a ridge appears around the edge, then pour off any surplus chocolate. Return to a cool place and leave until the chocolate is firm and has contracted enough to remove from the mould. This could take up to 2 hours.

To join the halves together, fill a piping bag with a No2 tube with melted chocolate and pipe a line of chocolate around the edge of one half. Join the two pieces together and support until the chocolate has set. A simpler method is to place one half of the egg on a heated baking tray for a few seconds and then quickly press it onto the other half.

Large Chocolate Easter Eggs

Use homemade chocolate eggs or purchased ones for these unusual Easter presents.

Egg with flowers

This egg can be created in a few minutes. Use melted chocolate to attach a spray of silk flowers to a chocolate egg and add ribbon trimming and a bow. Attach to a chocolate base, if wished. Any size chocolate egg is suitable, so long as the flowers and bow are kept in proportion.

Easter bunny egg

Roll out yellow marzipan and cut out a rabbit using a biscuit cutter. Stick with chocolate to the centre front of the egg. Cut out yellow marzipan flowers and make orange centres. Stick flowers over the join in the egg with melted chocolate.

Chocolate boats

Make half a chocolate egg. Make sails from rice paper and colour with dusting chalks. Dip the base of the sails in melted chocolate and attach to deck of boat. Cut out tiller and rudder from chocolate and attach with melted chocolate. Add modelled marzipan figures.

Chocolate cars

Make half a chocolate egg and turn onto the flat side. Using a heated 4cm (1½in) round cutter, cut a hole in the top.

Pour some melted chocolate onto greaseproof paper, then pick up and drop the paper several times to allow any air bubbles to burst. Place the half egg onto the melted chocolate. When the chocolate begins to set, cut around the egg with a sharp knife to form the base. Cut the wheels from chocolate and attach with melted chocolate. Use coloured sweets for hubcaps and headlamps. Decorate with coloured marzipan and royal icing. Add modelled rabbit.

Sugar Flowers

Moulded sugar flowers, so perfectly made that they look garden fresh, are an exquisite finishing touch for any celebration cake. In fact, an accomplished cake decorator can produce nearly every flower from flower paste, along with realistic buds and foliage. The fantastic wired flower arrangements here are a fine example of sugarart.

Flower Modelling

Wired, moulded sugar flowers have become much more common in recent years. Some people have described flower modelling as a new technique, but very fine flower modelling was done in the nineteenth century. More recent ideas, such as the wiring of flowers, the use of cutters and new pastes, have enabled the cake decorator to make finer, more delicate flowers.

Sugar flowers are made from flower paste, which is, of course, edible. However, if planning a cake with a floral spray, it is important to remember that the flowers are wired, and that the stamens are not edible. It is best to remove the spray or flowers to be kept as a reminder of a special occasion.

Basic shapes for flower modelling

Ball: Work a piece of paste until pliable, then place on the palm of your hand. Gently rotate it with the forefinger of the other hand to form a round ball.

Teardrop: Make a ball in the palm of your hand. Roll the forefinger backwards and forwards over half the ball to make the paste taper in a teardrop shape.

Baton: This is similar to a teardrop, but the stem is elongated and slender.

Cigar or Sausage: Make a ball, then roll the finger backwards and forwards along the length to form a narrow, cylindrical shape with rounded ends.

Golf tee: Make a teardrop, then pinch the broad end outwards to form a flat base.

Plug: Make a cigar and pinch one end to make a flattened base. The back should be rounded.

Teat: This is like a plug, but has an indentation behind the flattened section and a slight bulge towards the tip.

Methods of shaping petals and leaves

Before making moulded flowers, ensure that your hands are clean and dry. Wash your hands, dry them thoroughly, then work a tiny bit of cornflour into the palms. Brush off any cornflour sediment or the petals will dry out too quickly. Some cake decorators wear thin surgical gloves when making flowers.

Hand-shaping techniques

Softening: Place a cut-out petal onto the flattened palm of your hand. Run a ball tool gently but firmly around the outer edge of the petal. The ball should be half on and half off the petal. This lessens the cut look and gives a more natural flow to the petals.

Ruffling: Apply a bit more pressure with the ball tool to make the petal look slightly ruffled.

Soft frilling: Place the petal on your flattened palm. Apply strong pressure with the ball tool to make the petal look soft and smoothly frilled.

Cupping: Place the petal on your flattened palm. Using a ball tool and a circular motion, gently shape the petal, which should turn in the opposite direction to that in which the ball tool is moving.

Texturing: Lightly dust your thumb with cornflour and make a thumbprint in the centre of a petal to add soft lines.

Finger-shaping techniques

Balling: Place a small flower on the fingertip. Cup each petal, one at a time, by firmly pressing a ball tool into it.

Tweaking: Grasp a cut petal between thumb and forefinger, with the finger underneath and joints bent. Straighten the joints, which changes the pressure of the fingertips on the petal. Keep the thumb nearly still and quickly and firmly slide the forefinger along the petal, towards the thumb joint. When you let go, the petal will have stretched and curved.

Frilling: Tweak the petal, then place it on the tip of a forefinger coated with a little white fat. Firmly roll a cocktail stick from one edge to the other, along the outer edge, with the point of the stick in the centre of the flower.

Cutter flower techniques

Cupping: Use a small plunger cutter to shape the flower by ejecting it onto a piece of foam rubber which has been dusted with cornflour. The petals can be jabbed with a ball tool to make them more interesting.

Frilling: Place the cut petal on the board and roll over the edge with a cocktail stick to frill it. For a tight frill, roll backwards and forwards. For a more gentle frill, push the cocktail stick away in a steady, even movement.

Double frilling: Before frilling, cut the edge of the petal with small, regular cuts. The paste should be slightly thicker for a deep frill.

Equipment for Flower Modelling

In addition to the basic cake decorating equipment shown on page 10, moulded sugar flowers require some special tools. Start with the basic items shown here. A fishing tackle box or large sewing box is useful for storing equipment.

Polystyrene block: Use this for holding the flowers before they are wired into sprays.

Foam rubber: Many decorators work over a large square of thick foam rubber so that if a flower gets dropped it does not shatter. Smaller pieces of foam are needed for ejecting cutter flowers, for lifting and shaping petals and for protection while transporting finished sprays.

Wires: A selection of covered florist's wire in different gauges is needed. Use fine wire for small flowers and a heavier gauge for large flowers. Fine rose wire or fuse wire is useful for wiring together sprays.

Stamens: These come in many different shapes, sizes and colours.

Floral tape: Use this for covering wires and for assembling sprays.

Tape shredder: This is useful for cutting the floral tape into narrow strips.

Wire cutters: Use for cutting the florist's wire, or keep a pair of floristry scissors for the job.

Pliers: Use small long-nosed pliers for bending wire and electrical pliers for stripping wire.

Tweezers: Fine-pointed crank-ended craft tweezers are best for delicate work.

Cutters: There is a vast selection of petal and leaf cutters available.

Leaf formers: Rubber veiners designed for the pottery industry make realistic sugar leaves.

Glass-headed pins: These have a variety of uses in cake decorating. In flower modelling, they can be used like ball tools for small petals.

Confectioner's glaze: This is a special liquid which gives a shine to leaves and flowers.

Ribbons: All sugar flower sprays contain ribbons. Very narrow ones are best for this, and for ribbon insertion and banding. Wider ribbons can be used to cover cake boards.

Anger tool: Use for opening the throats of flowers.

Dresden pewter tool: This is useful for creating special effects, such as getting the right tilt to the large petal of a pansy.

Ribbed tool: Use for finger flowers.

Making Flower Paste

Although some cake decorating suppliers stock flower paste, it is preferable to make it. The flowers in this book have been made using the first recipe given here, but satisfactory results can be obtained from paste made by the second, easier recipe or from commercial pastes. Experiment until you find the paste you most enjoy working with.

Eight-sided Wedding Cake
This elegant sugarpasted cake features a sugar-flower spray of roses and freesias. The 23cm (9in) long cake is on a 33cm (13in) board. Wedding bell lace and delicate embroidery add to the summery effect.

Flower paste

This recipe is best if made using a heavy-duty mixer. An alternative method, using a hand-held electric mixer, is given, but it is much more difficult.

25ml (5 teaspoons) cold water
10ml (2 teaspons) powdered gelatine
450g (1lb/4 cups) icing sugar (confectioner's sugar)
15ml (3 teaspoons) gum tragacanth and 10ml (2 teaspoons) cornflower (cornstarch) or 10ml (2 teaspoons) gum tragacanth and 10ml (2 teaspoons) carboxy methyl cellulose.
10ml (2 teaspoons) liquid glucose
20ml (4 teaspoons) white vegetable fat (shortening)
white of 1 large egg with string removed

Method I (heavy-duty mixer)
Measure the cold water into an ovenproof container, sprinkle gelatine over surface and leave to stand for 1 hour.

Sift the icing sugar into the bowl of a heavy-duty mixer. Sprinkle the gum tragacanth and cornflower (or gum tragacanth and carboxy methyl cellulose) over the surface. Place in a preheated 100°C (200°F/gas mark ¼) oven for about 30 minutes to warm the sugar.

Warm the liquid glucose until it is runny. Dissolve the gelatine over hot but not boiling water. Remove from the heat and add the warmed glucose and the white fat. Return to low heat and stir until everything is dissolved and blended.

Heat the beater of the mixer in the oven or in hot water, dry and place it in the mixer. Place the bowl of warmed sugar in the mixer. Add the dissolved gelatine mixture and the egg white. Cover the bowl with a clean, dry cloth and turn the mixer to the slowest speed. Mix until all ingredients are combined. The paste will be a dull beige at this stage.

Turn the mixer to the maximum speed. Keeping your arm on the upper arm of the mixer, beat until the paste is very white and stringy.

Remove the paste from the bowl, place in a clean plastic bag, seal in an airtight container and refrigerate.

The paste must be left to mature for 24 hours before use.

Method II (hand-held electric mixer)
Place 225g (8oz/2 cups) of the icing sugar in a heatproof bowl. Add 10ml (2 teaspoons) cornflour (cornstarch) and the gum tragacanth (or gum tragacanth and carboxy methyl cellulose). Cover the bowl with a clean, dry cloth and place a plate on top. Place over a saucepan of boiling water and heat until the sugar is warm to the touch.

Sift the remaining icing sugar into an ovenproof bowl. Place in a preheated 100°C (200°F/gas mark ¼) oven until warm.

Dissolve the gelatine, glucose and white fat as in Method I.

Add the dissolved mixture and the egg white to the bowl over boiling water. Using a hand-held electric mixer, beat until the mixture becomes white and starts to thicken.

Gradually beat in the warmed sugar until the mixture becomes too thick to beat.

Turn any remaining icing sugar onto a work surface, add the beaten mixture and knead until all the sugar is incorporated into the paste.

Pack and store as in Method I.

Modelling paste
This paste is easier to make than the previous recipe. Experiment with different brands of sugarpaste to find one which works for you.

white vegetable fat (shortening)
225g (8oz) commercial sugarpaste
5ml (1 teaspoon) gum tragacanth

Rub white fat on your hands and knead together the sugarpaste and gum tragacanth until it is elastic.

Store in a plastic bag in an airtight container and rest for 24 hours before use. This paste keeps well if worked through about once a week.

Using flower paste
To work with flower paste made by either of these methods cut off a walnut-sized piece and knead until pliable. If the paste seems crumbly add small amounts of egg white and white fat until the right texture is reached.

When the paste is ready, it should 'talk': it will make a little clicking sound. It must reach the talking stage before cutting or moulding flowers.

Flower paste dries out quickly so never cut off more than a very tiny piece for use. A small piece goes a very long way, as it is rolled out very thinly.

Rose

The rose is the flower most often used on cakes. However, it is time consuming to make because of the number of petals.

Decide how many roses you want to make, so that all of the flower paste can be tinted at the same time. It is easier to work on several roses at the same time, so that each layer of petals has time to harden while you work on the next rose.

An easy way of colouring a rose is to make all the paste in a pale colour and then highlight the layers with petal dust. However, the most common method is to begin by tinting some paste in the deepest colour you want to use. Divide this piece in two, with one piece twice the size of the other. Set aside the small piece in the deepest colour, and add an equal quantity of white paste to the other piece. Continue dividing in this way until you have five tones of the original colour. The palest colour should have the largest amount.

Select the correct gauge of wire for the rose. If the wire is too thick it will be difficult to arrange the finished roses, but if it is too thin the roses will droop. Use 26-gauge for a medium-sized rose, 24-gauge for a large one. The size of the rose is determined by the size of the centre cone. The cutter should be 5mm (¼in) longer than the cone.

Take a small piece of the darkest paste, make a teardrop, and insert a hooked, moistened wire in the broad base. Use a thick knitting needle to roll the upper one-third away from the base to form a long, narrow band. Bend the band to form a right angle with the wire. Moisten the front with egg white and wind it round to create a spiralled centre. Do not worry if it looks untidy, as it should not be visible in the finished rose. Allow to dry completely before beginning to attach the petals.

An attractive rose needs five layers of petals. Layer 1 has one petal; Layer 2 has two interlocking petals; Layer 3 has two interlocking petals; Layer 4 has three petals; Layer 5 has five petals, these are cut from the larger cutter.

Layer 1: Roll out the paste until it is translucent and cut the petal with the smaller cutter. Place it in the palm of your hand and smooth, but do not frill, the edges with a ball tool. Moisten the lower two-thirds with a very light coating of egg white, position the cone 5mm (¼in) below the upper edge of the petal. Fasten tightly by rolling it into the centre with your thumb, then gently curve the edge of the petal with your finger.

Layer 2: Cut two petals with the small cutter. Soften the edge with a ball tool, then paint egg white onto the point of one petal. Place over the join of the petal in Layer 1, 2mm (⅛in) above it, and fasten down one side with your thumb. The opposite side will be free from the centre.

Insert the third petal into the gap between the cone and the second petal, matching the height of the petals. Wrap both petals tightly around the centre cone. To ensure a tight fit at the upper edge, slightly twist the petals down towards the base. This will create pleats on the base. Flatten them with your finger against the base, then gently furl back the petals a little.

Layer 3: Repeat the steps of Layer 2, but do not twist the petals to create pleats at the base. Instead, gently wrap the petals around the centre, opening out the top.

Layer 4: Cut petals with the small cutter. With a ball tool, soften and slightly frill the edge of each petal. Gently cup the first petal. With the point away from you, roll back one side with a cocktail stick. Cup the second petal and use a cocktail stick to curve back the upper edges in two sections, so that it looks like the brim of a stetson hat. Fasten onto the cone, overlapping the last petal by one third.

Cup the third petal and use a cocktail stick to roll back the opposite side to the one in the first petal in this layer. Fasten each petal onto the cone, overlapping each petal as you go. The final petal is arranged so the two curved edges meet without overlapping.

At this point, the flower is known as a half-rose, which is used frequently in the sprays. Add a calyx.

Layer 5: Cut five petals using the larger cutter. All of these petals are attached to the base of the flower, meeting around the wire.

Cup each petal and use a cocktail stick to curve them into natural-looking positions. Attach the first petal over the join between the two furled petals in Layer 4. Attach the other petals, overlapping to get a natural shape.

To prevent drooping petals, invert the flower, either by standing it upside down or by hanging the wire from something like a bent coat-hanger.

Calyx: It is important to make a calyx which is in proportion with the rose, so choose the right size calyx cutter for the flower. In nature, the rose calyx is large, but a botanically correct calyx might overwhelm a sugar rose.

Make a small ball of pale green flower paste and an equal-sized one in a deeper green. Press them together, then roll out on the board with the paler colour on the bottom. Cut the calyx and dust the inside with silver lustre colour.

To make a more realistic rose, remember that they have hair-like projections on some of the sepals of the calyx. If you want to add these, study a real rose to see where to place them.

Gently pierce the calyx with the wire and attach to the rose, placing the sepals over the joins between the petals. Make a tiny oval in the darker green paste to form the ovary. Brush the calyx with egg white and thread the ovary, and attach.

cone

layer 1

layer 2

layer 3

layer 4

half rose

layer 5

calyx

105

Briar Rose

This flower should be fairly large, and can it either be wired or unwired. They are usually wired if used on their own. If they are to be incorporated into a spray, arrange the spray so that the briar roses are added when the spray is in position.

There are two methods for making the centre. Either may be used, but do not make the mistake of mixing the methods on the same cake.

Method 1: Take a small ball of moist yellow paste. Press firmly against a piece of tulle to mark the surface. Insert a large number of stamens into this flattened, patterned knob. The stamens should be in multiples of five, and of various lengths. The shorter stamens should be towards the centre of the knob (it is essential to leave a bare patch in the middle) and the longer ones towards the outer edge, particularly at the junctions of the petals. A better effect is also obtained if the longer stamens are curved before inserted into the knob of paste. Allow this to dry before assembling the flower. Petal dust a deeper yellow around the outer edge. Touch the centre with a little greeny-yellow petal dust. Touch the tips of the stamens with the yellow petal dust and highlight each stamen with a touch of brown paste colour.

Method 2: Take ordinary cotton sewing thread and run it through your fingers dusted with yellow petal dust. Bind it round the forefinger about 30 times. Bind with a piece of 28-gauge wire. Cut the threads opposite the wire. Spray with starch, spread sideways and curve over finger until a good shape is achieved. Repeat this three times. Interlock the three bunches together so they overlap, and bind tightly together with stemfix. Ensure that the circles of thread look as though they are a whole, not divided into separate pieces. Use sharp scissors to shorten some of the pieces of thread so that you have the impression of having long and short stamens.

Take a tiny piece of yellow paste, make a golf tee and fasten this into the centre, disguising the joins between the bunches of thread. Ensure the threads are spread and curved. Use a small pair of scissors to cut some of the inner threads shorter than the outer threads. Tint the centre and the threads with

saffron yellow petal dust. Highlight the centre with green petal dust. Tip the ends of the threads with a touch of brown paste colour.

Roll out a piece of green paste until it is translucent. Cut out a shape with the calyx cutter. Cut tiny, hairlike threads on the edges of the sepals as for the rose. Place in the centre of an apple tray coated with a little white fat and dust with silver lustre colour.

Roll out pale pink paste until translucent. Cut five petals with rose petal cutters or with a heart-shaped cutter. If using rose petal cutters, cut a notch in the rounded end with the V-shaped point of the same cutter, and neaten with a pair of curved scissors. Soften the edges of the petals with the medium-sized ball tool, without frilling the petals. Using the large ball tool cup the petals.

Paint a touch of egg white in the centre of the calyx and along two adjoining sepals. Place the V-shaped point of the petal to the centre of the calyx, with the edge of the petal in line with the outer edges of the sepals. Continue placing the petals in the calyx, matching the petal edges with the sepals. Place the final petal on top of the first.

If the flower is to be wired, make an opened hook in one end of a piece of 24-gauge wire. Now bend this to a 90° angle. Paint a little egg white on the centre of the petals, and gently pull the circle into place. The wire should be inserted off centre so that the circle of wire is in the centre of the flower. Paint a little more egg white on the wire, and place the knob containing the stamens over the wire. Fasten a paper clip onto the wire so that it holds the apply tray firmly.

If using the thread method, tape together the three wires to form the stem. Moisten the centre of the petals with egg white and gently pull the centre into place. Use a paper clip to hold the apply tray firmly in place.

To finish the flower, move the petals into realistic positions, and hold in place with small pieces of foam rubber. Curl the sides or edges of some of the petals with a cocktail stick. When the flower is dry, petal dust the base of each petal with yellow, and then touch the edges with a deeper pink.

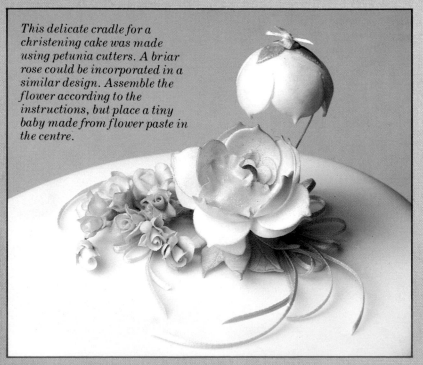

This delicate cradle for a christening cake was made using petunia cutters. A briar rose could be incorporated in a similar design. Assemble the flower according to the instructions, but place a tiny baby made from flower paste in the centre.

assembled petals

centre (method 2)

calyx with first petal

centre　　　　*layer 1*　　　　　　*layer 2*

Sweet Pea

These flowers come in a lovely selection of colours: red, pink, cerise, purple, mauve and white. They look best in a cluster and not mixed with other flowers.

You will need sweet pea cutters, a small star calyx cutter, a small rose petal cutter and 28-gauge wire.

Make a rounded hook at the end of the wire, leaving a gap in the centre. Fill this gap with a small piece of paste, taking care to cover the wire. The centre of the gap should be slightly rounded.

Layer 1: Roll the paste to a medium thickness for the keel. Cut one petal with the rose petal cutter. Gently smooth the cut edges with a ball tool. Brush a fine coating of egg white over the petal. Place the padded wire onto the petal with the straight edge of the wire along the centre of the petal, with the point aiming down the wire. Gently close the petal around the padded centre. Make a neat edge. There should be no opening visible. Firmly grasp the wire in your right hand and the tip of the petal in your left hand,

and gently tip back the petal so it is slightly curved.

Layer 2 (wings): Roll out the paste very finely. Cut one shape with the wing cutter. Gently frill the petal in the palm of your hand with a ball tool for a soft-looking flower. If making a more frilly flower, frill on the board with a cocktail stick. The frill lines should go right to the centre of the flower, giving an almost fluted appearance.

Paint a little egg white onto the point. Fasten this to the base of the keel. The tipped-back keel should protrude through the slit in the wings. Although using only one cutter shape, there are actually two petals in this layer.

Outer petal (standard): This petal should be translucent or the flower

will look very heavy. Cut one petal. Mark a line down the centre with a cocktail stick or veining tool, from the top to the point. Frill the petal either on the palm of the hand or with a cocktail stick so that it matches the wings. Paint a little egg white onto the point and attach this to the base of the wings. Pinch firmly. Reinforce the line marked by pinching the back of the petal to form a ridge. Paint a spot of egg white at the upper edge of the petal on the ridge and pinch the petal together firmly. Very gently tip backwards to make it look realistic.

Calyx: Make a tiny golf tee with green paste. Roll out the paste very thinly. Cut out one shape with the tiny star cutter. With the head of a glass-headed pin, make an

108

outer petal

indentation in the centre of the calyx. Paint a little egg white into the hollow, insert the wire through the hollow and gently nestle the flower into the cupped calyx.

Buds: When making a bud follow the procedure for making a flower until completing the keel section, using very pale green paste (this will be petal dusted later to give the colour needed). Using the same paste, cut one petal with the rose petal cutter. Mark a line down the centre of the petal with the veiner or cocktail stick, as for the standard petal on the complete flower, and soften the edges of the petal on the palm of the hand with a ball tool. Paint a little egg white onto the point of the second petal, and stick it to the keel where it emerges from

the wire. The front edge of this petal should be a tiny bit longer than the completed keel. Reinforce the ridge as before, lifting the petal slightly at the same time.

Make a calyx as before, fastening it to the flower as above. For realism, gently curve the wire so that the keel is bent towards the stem. Look at a picture of a sweet pea, or at the real thing to get this arch right. It makes a fantastic difference to the final look of the spray of flowers. It is usual to incorporate about five buds into a spray of sweet peas on a head, and about three complete flowers.

The leaves are long ovals, with veins curving in to the centre of the leaf at the base. Some are slightly ruffled at the edges.

Add tendrils. These actually appear below the leaves, which are arranged in pairs, but on sugar flowers they look attractive fastened below the junction of the buds. Take a strip of stemtex that has been cut into four. Attach it firmly to the wire below the buds. Cut it into two. Gently grasp the end of one piece and twist gently. It will form a straight, tight thread. Do the same to the second piece of stemtex. Holding the wire in your right hand, hold a cocktail stick horizontal with the same hand. Now twist the thread around the cocktail stick until you have formed a neat tendril. Gently pull the cocktail stick out, and arrange the tendril so it doesn't look too rigid. Repeat for the second one.

Carnation

A sugar carnation is a spectacular flower which impresses many people. Tint all the paste a delicate pastel colour so that the finished flower can then be tinted with petal dust. If making deep red carnations, it is better to make the paste a deep orangy-red and then add further colour with petal dust. Deep coloured flowers require the addition of a good deal of colour, which increases the sensitivity to moisture and damage.

Remove the tips of a white stamen, and fold in half. Position alongside a piece of 26-gauge wire, with the cut ends level. Bind the stamen to the wire with a fine piece of rose wire, and trim off any projecting wire. Coat the dampened knot with a tiny piece of paste. Using scissors or tweezers, bend the stamens in an arc, separating them slightly at the tips.

Layer 1: Roll out a piece of paste until it is fairly thin, and cut one layer at a time with a carnation cutter. At each scallop make a cut about 5mm (¼in) deep. Along the outer edge of each curve make many slashes with a modelling knife. These slashes will enable you to get the lovely jagged edge of the carnation. This is called double frilling. When you start frilling, lift one petal and roll a cocktail stick firmly backward and forward along the edge of the petal next to the lifted one.

When you have frilled the entire circumference of the layer, brush a little egg white onto the centre up to the long cuts between the scallops. Insert the wire and stamens through the centre of the circle, fold the circle in half, just allowing the stamens to peep over the top, frilled edge. You now have a semicircle.

Carefully brush a little egg white onto the right half of the semicircle. Fold the right-hand edge to the centre, ensuring that the frilled edges are level. Gently touch the fold to make the sections stick together. Turn the flower over so that the flap is to the right. Brush on a little egg white and fold the right-hand side over, level with the far edge, ensuring that the upper frilled edge is level. The circle is now divided into six in a closed Z-shape. Using the forefingers and thumbs of both hands, gather the base of the semicircle together, making sure you cannot see the join of the stamens and wire or the folds of the flower.

Layer 2: Make the same as Layer 1 up to the point where you brush on the egg white. A little less egg white is needed for this layer. Insert the wire into the centre of the circle. Invert the flower onto the palm of your hand and gently push the petal down onto the existing petal. The base of the first petal should protrude very slightly through the centre of the second.

wired stamen

layer 1

110

Gather the petal together with the fingers of your working hand. Don't press down firmly or you will break off delicate pieces from the first layer. Turn the flower the right way up, slimming down the base.

Layer 3: Make exactly as Layer 2. Dry hanging upsidedown, or the layers will become noticeable.

Calyx: To make the calyx, roll a large pea-size ball of pale apple green paste. Roll into a teardrop, and pinch the broad end sideways between fingers and thumbs so that you have the rough outline of a golf tee. Place the flattened piece on a work surface and roll out the paste until very fine. Cut with a small rose calyx cutter. Invert this over the stem of the golf tee. Insert a small ball tool into the centre of the calyx, expanding it a little, and rounding the base. The sepals of the calyx should be pushed upwards so they are in line.

Moisten the inside of the calyx and sepals with a little egg white. Insert the base of the flower into the calyx, making sure the wire protrudes through the base, and fasten. Invert the flower, and with a small pair of curved scissors make four small nicks round the base of the calyx. Do not cut them off, leave them attached. Roll a cocktail stick from the attached section of the nicks to the tips, so they lie against the calyx again.

To make leaves take a very small ball of green paste. Roll it into a cigar shape, giving it sharply pointed tips. Roll a knitting needle along the cigar from the centre to the tip. Leave a small thickened section in the centre. Insert the wire through the centre. When the paste reaches the position where you want the leaf, dampen the wire with a little egg white, and pinch the leaf onto the wire. Curve the first two leaves upwards. Alternating the pairs of leaves at 180° angles, curve the others gently downwards. Petal dust the finished flower.

layer 2

layer 3

calyx

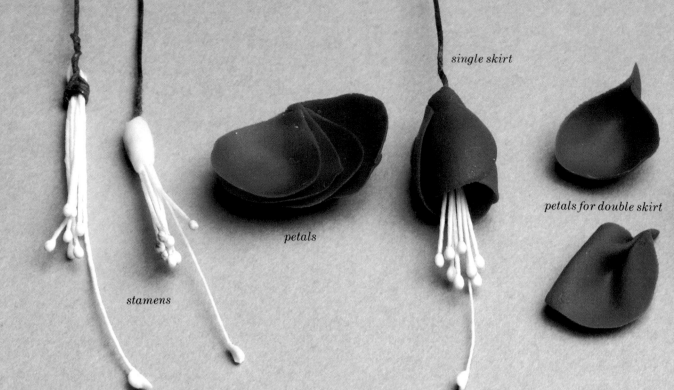

single skirt

petals for double skirt

petals

stamens

Fuchsia

This very attractive flower is most spectacular when used on cakes, but it must be arranged so that it hangs. The beauty of the flowers can be lost if they are arranged flat on the surface of a cake. Fuchsias can be made as either a single or a double variation.

The stamens and first layer of petals are made exactly the same for both varieties.

Take four small stamens and fold them in half so you have eight stamens gathered together. They should not be completely even in length, but should not vary too greatly. Take one larger, white stamen and arrange it to come from the centre of the other stamens. It should protrude by about 2-2.5cm (¾-1in).

Take a piece of 28-gauge wire and hold it so that it is the same length as the stamens. Bind the long end of the wire around the folded stamens three times. Trim off the excess sections of the stamens, and bind the short piece of wire around the long piece, forming a secure centre. Cover the knot with a tiny piece of paste to give the first layer of petals something to adhere to.

Skirt: Cut four petals with the smallest rose petal cutter. Soften the edge of each petal with a ball tool and then gently cup each petal. They should not be very cupped.

Dampen the point of the first petal with a little egg white, and take the egg white along the right-hand edge of the petal for a short distance. Place the second petal on top of the first, overlapping the petal by about two-thirds. Moisten the second petal in the same way as the first and then position the third petal. Each petal should meet exactly at the tip. Repeat the process for the fourth petal. There will be a fan shape of four petals with all the tips meeting in the same place. Paint a little egg white along the edge of the right-hand petal. Place the stamens on the petals, allowing them to protrude well beyond the broad edge of the petals. The stamens should be arranged right at the left-hand edge of the fan. Using a cocktail stick, cover the stamens with the petals, and roll up the four petals so that a neat spiral is created. If making a single fuchsia, add the sepals at this stage.

If making a double fuchsia you now move on to the second layer. Cut four petals the same size as the previous layer. Soften the edge of each petal with a ball tool and cup it. Pinch the pointed tip of the petal firmly so that the edges stick to one another. The petal should have a shovel shape. Repeat this process for each petal in the layer. Dampen the join between two petals on the first layer, and position a petal so that it covers the join. Repeat the process until each petal is in place over the join of the previous layer.

For the third layer, cut another four petals the same size. Soften the edge of each petal with the ball tool and then cup each petal gently. Gather the pointed end of each petal, curling back one side of the petal over a cocktail stick. Repeat this process for all four petals in the layer. Position each of these petals on moistened joins of the previous layer. Set the skirt aside to dry.

Sepals: The sepals should be a contrasting colour to the skirt, and the same colour as the stamens.

Take a medium-sized ball of paste, turn it into a teat, flatten the lower edge and cut out one shape with the fuchsia cutter. The paste should be rolled out very thinly, and the pedestal should be narrower immediately behind the sepals. The back of the pedestal should be kept rounded. Soften each edge of the sepals with a ball tool. Place the calyx on the palm of your hand and

double fuchsia   *triple fuchsia*

sepals

stroke each sepal in turn with a small ball tool from the point to the centre so that the sepals curve gracefully. Make a small indentation in the base of the calyx with either a small ball tool or the tip of a skewer, moisten the hollow with egg white and then pull in the skirt so that it fits into the calyx.

Take a small ball of green paste, roll it into an oval and thread this onto the wire. Add a touch of egg white to the base of the calyx and pull the bead into place, retaining the oval shape. For more realism, the ovary should be glazed with confectioner's glaze.

If making fuchsias with their leaves, remember that the veins and most stems are red.

113

wired sepals

wired petals

tongue

column

assembly method II

114

Cattleya Orchid

This is the traditional American bridal orchid, and it looks very attractive on a cake.

There are two distinct ways of making this orchid. The first is easier to assemble, but difficult to insert into a spray because the petals are inflexible and break easily. The second method involves wiring each petal, which makes it easier to wire the flowers into a spray.

The flower is divided into the column, the tongue, side petals and sepals. The column and tongue are made the same, whatever mode of assembly you decide upon.

Column: Gently curve the end of a piece of 24-gauge wire. Moisten with egg white. Take a small ball of white paste. Turn this into a teardrop and insert the curved wire into the narrow point of the teardrop. Make sure this is tightly fastened to the wire. Curve the teardrop to follow the curve of the wire. See that the tip of the teardrop protrudes beyond the end of the wire. Using a very sharp modelling knife, gently slice the tip of the teardrop in two places, on either side of the wire. The centre should be broader than the other segments.

Using your thumbs, gently hollow the underside of the column. Pinch the two side segments, curve the broad centre section downwards, curve the outer segments inward so they overlap the central part.

The column must be slender and gently curved. Allow to dry. If making a coloured flower, dust the column in a paler shade than the rest of the flower.

Tongue: This should always be made at least 24 hours before assembling the flower. Roll out a piece of paste until it is the right thickness for frilling. Cut out one tongue shape. Texture the upper surface of the tongue with an orchid former, a cocktail stick, or with a veiner. Frill the edges of the petal, tapering the frill towards the V-shaped point.

Paint a little egg white onto the lower 2cm (¾in) of the V-shaped point. Pick up the dried column and place it on top of the tongue with the wire protruding from the V-shaped end. Make sure the column tip is pointing down. Join the two sides together where you have applied the egg white as if starting a French seam. Hold the tongue in your right hand with the finger and thumb on either side of the French seam, over the column. With the forefinger and thumb of the left hand, carefully push back the frilled edge of the tongue against the thumb and finger of the right hand. Gently tug down the tip of the tongue, curving it over a skewer. Leave to dry.

Petals (Unwired): Cut two petals with the broader cutter. Fold the first petal in half, and firmly pinch in a ridge. Open up the petal and frill with a cocktail stick. The petals are not frilled as much as the tongue. Place over a tube while you work on the second petal and the sepals. Repeat on the opposite side for the second petal. The ridges must be at the top.

Sepals (Unwired): Cut three long narrow shapes. Gently soften the edges. With a veining tool or a ball tool hollow the sepals from the tip to the centre. They will curve slightly.

Assembly Method I: Lightly grease a polystyrene apple cup. Place the first sepal in place, with the point to the edge of the cup and the rounded end in the centre. Apply a little egg white to the centre. Lap the second sepal (broad end) over the first, then add the third to make an upsidedown Y-shape.

Apply a little egg white to the centre again, place the first of the two petals onto the centre, with the points curving outwards and downwards. Add a little more egg white and position the second petal. Add a little more egg white and place the wire of the dried tongue in the centre of the join. Gently pull this through the five layers of paste, and through the polystyrene cup. Tug hard so the tongue and column bury themselves into the soft paste. Place a paper clip across the underside of the apple cup to hold it firmly in place. Allow to dry after arranging the petals. Petal dust as required, remembering the saffron yellow throat.

Petals (Wired): Strip approximately 2cm (¾in) of tape off two pieces of 28-gauge wire. Take a small ball of paste, turn it into a teardrop and with a thick knitting needle roll out the first petal from the centre, leaving a thickened ridge down the centre. The rest of the petal should be translucent. Cut out the petal. Reinforce a ridge down the centre of the petal, having it uppermost. Frill the edge of the petal. Moisten the stripped section of wire with a little egg white. Insert this into the ridge so that the wire is not visible from either side. Drape the petal over a curved object and leave to dry. Repeat the process for the second petal, remembering to curve it in the opposite direction from the first, still ridge uppermost. Leave to dry.

Sepals (Wired): Strip approximately 2cm (¾in) tape off three pieces of 28-gauge wire. Take a ball of paste, roll it into a cigar and roll out the sepal, leaving a ridge in the centre. Cut out the sepal with the narrow cutter. Moisten the stripped piece of wire with egg white. Insert into the thickened ridge, and then hollow the petal from the tip to the centre, without exposing the wire. Place this over a curve to dry, hollow on the inside of the curve. Repeat to make two more sepals.

Assembly Method II: All pieces must be very dry. Highlight the petals and sepals with petal dust as desired, remembering to highlight the inner throat with saffron yellow.

Assemble the orchid using fine rose wire. The tongue forms the centre of the flower. Wire the two frilled petals onto the central column on either side and slightly to the rear of the tongue. Ensure that the petals curve up and away from the tongue, and that the ridge remains on the upper surface of each petal. Next bind the dorsal sepal firmly into place, and finally, one by one, the lateral sepals. When assembling orchids this way you have a greater choice of the flow of the petals. You may also re-arrange the petals once they are inserted into the spray so that they look natural.

Selection of Flowers

The following pages give instructions for making many of the most commonly used sugar flowers.

Daffodil

This popular flower comes in many shapes, sizes, colours and varieties. Here is a simple way of creating an attractive, decorative flower.

The flower is divided into the trumpet, skirt and sheath. You will need a set of daffodil cutters; a small arum lily cutter; seven stamens; and 28-gauge wire.

Take three stamens without tips, and one with a tip, which should protrude slightly above the others. Place a piece of wire alongside the stamens, with a loose end protruding well in front of the tipped stamen. Bind the longer length of wire tightly around the stamens, close to the tip. The trumpet is not very deep and the stamens do not usually protrude beyond it. Turn back the protruding wire and bind around the longer piece. Trim the protruding piece neatly.

Roll out a piece of paste, allowing a little thickness for frilling. Using a cocktail stick, gently press lines onto the surface, to make a slightly corrugated effect. Apply a little egg white to one of the shorter sides of the trumpet. Wrap the trumpet around until the two shorter edges are joined together. It helps to use the end of a paint brush or the tip of a skewer inside the trumpet while you are doing this. Press the join firmly. If you have smoothed out some of your corrugations replace them with a cocktail stick.

The trumpet now has a narrow end and a broad end. Using a cocktail stick, firmly frill the broad edge. Tip back gently. Gather the narrow end between your fingers and thumb to draw it in, moistening the narrow end a little so it gathers together.

Make a very small ball of green paste, and drop into the trumpet. Using the end of a paint brush or the tip of a skewer, gently press the green ball onto the gathered base of the trumpet. Pull the wired stamens into the centre of the trumpet, being careful not to lose the gathered look. Imbed the stamens into the small green ball. Allow to dry.

Take a medium-sized ball of paste. Turn it into a teardrop, pinch the broad end flat into a golf tee shape, leaving a long, elegant, tapering point. Place the flattened part onto the board, and use a knitting needle to roll out the paste until translucent, being careful not to distort the upright point, and not developing a thick ring at the base of the point. Place the cutter over the point, making sure the base is centred, and cut it out. Hold the petals with the point resting between your fingers. Carefully, one petal at a time, soften the edges, hollow very gently, and mark with a veining tool.

Roll out another piece of paste the same colour and cut out another shape. With a small ball tool make a shallow indentation in the base. Soften the edges with a ball tool, cup gently and mark with a veining tool. Apply a little egg white to the

indentation in the base. Cross the second layer of petals over the first so that they are interspersed. Gently fix the upper layer to the base, remaking the indentation with the ball tool. Apply a little egg white to the indentation, carefully inserting the wire from the trumpet down through the centre.

Take a small piece of green paste, roll into a ball and then into an oval; thread this onto the wire and fasten it to the tip of the base with a little egg white. Gently work this onto the point so it appears to be part of it and not 'stuck on'. This forms the ovary. Carefully cover the wire with a coating of paste, giving a more realistic look to the stem. Before the paste dries, carefully bend the daffodil at the point where the ovary and the stem meet. Cut out a greeny-brown, very fine shape with the small arum lily cutter. Gather it gently after softening the edges with a ball tool to create a realistic look. Attach to the stem just below the bend. This forms the sheath.

Cymbidium Orchid

This very brightly coloured flower is sometimes used in bridal sprays. It can also be made in unusual bronze or green colours. The flower is divided into the column, the tongue, side petals and sepals.

As with the cattleya orchid there are two ways of making this flower: the petals can either be fixed or wired.

The column is made the same way for both methods. Gently curve the end of a piece of 24-gauge wire. Take a small ball of paste, slightly paler than the petals. Turn this into a teardrop and insert the curved wire, which has been moistened with egg white, into the narrow point of the teardrop. Ensure that the column is tightly fastened to the wire. Curve the teardrop to follow the curve of the wire. The tip of the teardrop must protrude beyond the end of the wire. Using your thumbs and forefingers gently mould the column. It should be hollow underneath, and have a slight ridge on the upper, curved section. The front of the column should be rounded with two shallow indentations on either side of the wire.

Take a tiny piece of white paste, make a tiny ball. Moisten it with egg white and fasten it firmly to the underside of the tip of the column. Using a cocktail stick, firmly press an indentation into the centre of the ball so that it almost splits it in two. Before proceeding any further with the orchid the column should be tinted as is required to complete the orchid. There are tiny spots on the underside of the column and these should be painted on with paste colour now. Allow to dry completely before continuing.

Tongue The tongue should be made at least 24 hours before assembling the flower. Cut one petal shape. Gently smooth the edges of the two rounded side pieces. Using an orchid former or a plastic leaf with parallel veining, gently texture the petal. With a medium-sized ball tool gently stroke the side pieces until they curve.

Take a small piece of saffron coloured paste, roll it into a ball, then a cigar, and flatten with a cocktail stick. The shape should gently taper at one end. Moisten with egg white and position it on the centre of the tongue, protruding slightly for-

wards from the two side pieces. Frill the edge of the front curve.

Moisten the back point of the tongue with egg white and attach to the column. The two curved side pieces should be about level with the top of the column, or slightly higher if you prefer, but do not close over the column, as in the cattleya orchid. Bend the front frilled edge of the tongue downwards in a graceful curve. Set aside to dry. When the tongue is dry, tint as required.

Side petals (unwired)
Cut one shape of the petals. Remove one of the three petals. Smooth the edges with the ball tool. Mark a ridge on the centre of each petal and use a ball tool to curve the petal, shaping it at the same time. Place in an apple tray to hold the shape while you work on the sepals.

Sepals (unwired)
Cut one shape, and smooth all the edges with a ball tool. Stretch the central petal (dorsal petal) with a ball tool until it is broader and longer than the other two. The dorsal petal should be curved in the centre and at the sides. It should curve backwards in the centre, but

once you have done this turn the shape over and gently run your ball tool down the sides of the petal, just inside the edge so that the sides turn backwards slightly.

Curve the two lower petals backwards by using the ball tool on the back. Set this into an apple tray. On this occasion you need a tray that has not been cut into individual cups. The top (dorsal) petal curves forwards and the two lower petals curve backwards, and the apple tray should support it in this position. Tint the petals.

Place a little egg white in the centre of the shape. Place the two side petals across the other shape as shown. Add a little more egg white into the centre and pull the set tongue and column firmly to the centre of the other five petals, with the column just below the dorsal petal.

If you want to make the cymbidium, with the petals wired individually, proceed as before with the column and the tongue. Tint these pieces as required.

The cutters for wiring the petals separately are slightly different:

the dorsal petal cutter is larger than the cutter to be used for the other petals. If working on all the petals together, roll out a fairly long piece of paste with one long side thicker than the other. The flat edges are all cut into this thick piece.

Cover all the cut pieces with plastic and work on one petal at a time, starting with the dorsal petal. Strip a piece of 28-gauge wire about 2cm (¾in) long. Moisten the bare wire with egg white and insert it into the thick piece of paste. Smooth the edges with a ball tool. Cup the centre of the petal along the length of it, working from the wired end to the tip. Once a gentle cupped curve has been achieved turn the petal over and with the ball tool just inside the edge, using a little pressure, make the edge curve backwards. Set over a curve and leave to dry.

Work on each of the other petals one at a time. The two side (lateral) petals have a ridge down the centre, and curve backwards slightly. The side edges can be softened, not frilled. The petals should be set over a curve to dry. The ridge should be away from the curve. The two lower petals are gently cupped and curved. Place over a curve to dry, with the cupped side towards the curve. When all the petals are dry tint them.

To assemble, start with the tongue. Use a couple of twists of rose wire around each petal wire, one at a time, to hold it firmly in place. Don't bind the wire in a downward spiral, keep it in as tight a coil as possible. Don't twist the separate petal wires around one another, as this makes it more difficult to reposition the petals of the complete flower.

Wire the two side petals slightly behind the tongue, with the ridges pointing forward. The lowest edges of the petals should be in a line, so that the petals don't end up at different heights.

Wire in the dorsal petal behind the lateral petals, and centred between them, behind the column. Position the two lower petals. Curve petals up or down as wished.

Cut off the petal wires 2cm (¾in) down. Leave the wire of the column intact. Tape all the wires to the column wire very tightly and neaten the flower. When positioning the orchid in a spray, remember that the petals are long and very brittle.

Peruvian Lily (Alstroemeria)

This very brightly coloured flower is often used in bridesmaids' bouquets and adds great emphasis to a spray.

Cut the heads off one end of each of three large and three small white stamens. Line up the tip of a piece of 28-gauge wire with the heads of the stamens. Hold tightly while binding the long end of the wire around the base of the stamens three times. Bend the remaining piece of wire back down towards the stem and bind this tightly around the stem. Cut off any excess wire. Cover the knot with a small piece of paste. Bend the heads of the stamens at a 45° angle. Colour the three large stamens a deep olive green. The others should be creamy yellow, or tone with the colour of the large petals.

Roll out a piece of paste and cut three petals with a narrow daisy petal cutter. Mark down the centre with a veining tool. Pinch the back of each petal to emphasise the central fold. Pinch the tips to a sharp point. Cover the petals with a piece of plastic, and quickly tint.

Paint on the spots and stripes.

Attach the petals to the stamens with a little egg white painted on in a V-shape, slightly overlapping the two petals that are to one side. The stamens should lean towards the single petal, but the bent heads point away towards the join between the two opposite petals. Curve the petals back, and allow to dry.

Make a golf tee of paste and roll out so it is translucent. Cut three large petals using a tulip cutter. Press the upper surface of the petal gently to the palm of your hand. This will give a soft tracery of veins. Turn the petal over and, with a veining tool, mark a vein down the centre of the petal. Ruffle the edge of the petal gently using a medium-sized ball tool. Turn over and reinforce the central vein by pinching the petal to a ridge. Run the ball tool down the petal from the upper edge to the point on either side of the ridge. This will curve the petal backwards. Pinch the ridge very firmly between your fingers at the upper edge of the petal pulling it backwards at the same time. Attach to the central petals so that they overlap slightly and fit behind the gaps. The last petal to be attached should be the one opposite the single petal in the first layer. Make a neat trumpet shape at the base.

Tint the petals as desired, but be sure to tip the point on the outer petals olive green. The green extends down the ridge at the back of the petal. Bend the stem wire to a 45° angle, with the single petal in the inner layer pointing down.

The buds are torpedo-shaped, with three ridges, bronze in colour, with green stripes and accentuations. The leaves are oval, slightly ruffled with clear veining. The tip of each leaf should be pinched and tinted a creamy yellow. The leaves are very glossy. Glaze with gum arabic solution or confectioner's glaze.

Italian Bellflower (Campanula)

This is a small, neat flower that will enhance any spray that needs a touch of blue.

Colour the paste a very pale blue. Take a piece of paste the size of a pea. Roll into a small ball, then into a teardrop. Using a skewer or anger tool, make a small hole in the centre. Hollow slightly. Cut into five

even petals with a fine pair of scissors. Pinch the tips of the petals between finger and thumb to make a sharp point. Tweak each petal to form elegant ovals. The petals should be narrower at the junction point than midway up. Each petal should be pointed.

The back of the flower is fairly shallow, so cut off any excess paste. Place the flower, petal-side down on the palm of your hand. Softly cup the underside of the petal, and curve the tip upwards. Invert the flower. Gently cup the centre, and use a veining tool to mark a shallow groove in the centre of each petal.

Place a tiny ball of white paste onto the stem of a white stamen, about 2cm (¾in) from the tip. Insert the stamen into the centre of the

flower, moisten with a little egg white. Pull the stamen with ball of paste attached through the centre until the ball of paste rests against the centre of the flower.

Make a tiny calyx using the smallest blossom cutter. Roll out pale green paste very thinly; cut the calyx, trimming the rounded tips of the petals with a modelling knife, or by pinching them. The flowers are attached to the plant stems in pairs.

Leaves are a glossy dark green, similar to violet leaves in shape, but more fluted. Roll a medium-sized ball of paste into a teardrop. Place this on your work surface. Flatten slightly. Roll out the leaf sideways from the centre leaving a central thickened ridge. Cut out a leaf with a heart-shaped cutter. Place the leaf on the palm of your hand and soften the cut edges with a ball tool. Using a piece of 28-gauge covered wire, strip 1cm (⅜in) of covering from the wire. Moisten the bare wire with a little egg white and insert this into the central ridge, making sure the wire cannot be seen.

Vein the leaf with a rose leaf mould. Invert the veined side of the petal onto the palm of your hand and with a small ball tool softly flute the leaf between the veins. Curl the edges of the petals by running the small ball tool gently inside the underside of the leaf. Petal dust the leaves and gloss with confectioner's glaze.

When making buds form a small ball of pale blue paste. Turn it into a teardrop. Insert a stamen into the centre, fastening the bud firmly to the stem of the stamen. Slash the teardrop from the broad end of the teardrop to the point making three petals. Grasp the point of the bud and twist slightly. Make a small calyx as for the flower and attach this to the bud.

To make a partially open bud repeat the process to where you have just slashed the bud. Insert the blade of the knife into one side of each petal and prise it slightly open. Pinch this between thumb and forefinger. Grasp the tip of the bud and twist gently. If you lose the slashes reinforce them. This twisting gives a pretty spiral effect to the bud. Make a small calyx or paint one onto the bud.

Gypsophila

This very delicate flower is used as a filler behind more substantial flowers.

Use a 30-gauge wire. If it is covered but not coloured, tint it green by running the wire through fingers covered with green petal dust.

Take desiccated (shredded) coconut, put it into a blender and turn to maximum. When the coconut is very fine switch off the machine and then rub the coconut through a fine sieve.

Make very small hooks on the end of short pieces of wire. Make small round knobs of flowerpaste on the end of each wire. Dip each knob into egg white (about two-thirds should be moist) and then into the sieved coconut. When the knobs are dry, petal dust the bases green. Tape several knobs together into small clusters, following the pattern created by the real flowers.

Freesia

This beautiful flower is used in many bridal bouquets so is very useful for a cake decorator to be able to make it.

Take three small white stamens. Cut them in half. Remove the head from one end. Dampen this end with water for about 5mm (¼in). Flatten it by pressing the stamen on your board with a palette knife. Cut the flattened end into three tiny threads with a small pair of scissors. Spread these threads out from one another. Bind this pistil together with the three white stamens using a piece of 28-gauge wire. Cover the knot with a small piece of paste.

You will need a small tulip cutter to complete the flower. Take a large pea-sized piece of paste. Roll into a teardrop shape and then flatten to form a plug shape. Roll out the base until fine. Place the cutter over the central knob and cut out the petal. With the cone-shaped tool open the throat of the flower, keeping the shape of a freesia.

Using the pad of your finger, elongate the three petals of the flower with a medium-sized ball tool, gently cupping the petals at the same time. Mark parallel lines onto the upper surface of each petal. Place this piece under an inverted glass so that it will remain pliable while you work on the second layer.

Take a small piece of paste. Make a very short teardrop and flatten it to make a golf tee shape with a very short back. Open the throat of this layer as before, gently elongating and cupping the petals as for the previous layer. Place the cone-shaped tool into the throat of this layer, gently dip the pinted end into egg white and insert this into the throat of the previous layer.

The petals should be arranged so that those of the first layer fit between those of the second layer. With your fingers, gently squeeze the two layers of petals together to make a single tubular flower. Mark parallel lines on the petals of the second layer.

Pull the stamens into the centre of the flower and arrange the petals. There should be a slender base to the flower, below the bulbous base. Cut a diamond-shaped sepal and fasten to the base of the flower with a little egg white.

Singapore Orchid

This is a very dainty orchid, often used in bridal sprays. They come in a variety of colours, some vibrant and some very delicate.

Take a medium-sized ball of paste and roll it into a teardrop. Maintaining the thickened point, roll out the broad edge of the teardrop until it is fine. Using a cutter or a pair of scissors, cut to the desired shape. Gently curve the tongue into the required position and texture as desired. Some orchids have strong markings on the tongue.

Take a piece of 28-gauge wire and make a small column on the slightly curved edge of the wire. Insert this into the centre of the prepared tongue, making sure that the wire protrudes through the thickened tip of the tongue in the correct position for this flower. Set this aside to dry.

Strip the ends of five more pieces of 28-gauge wire. Cut two triangular lateral petals, either with a cutter or using a template. Texture them as desired. They should have fairly strong veins showing. Insert

a stripped piece of moistened wire into the base of each petal. Drape them over an appropriate curve to dry.

Cut three long, narrow sepals from the paste using a cutter. With a veining tool, mark a strong central vein down the centre of each of these petals. Arrange the two lower petals over a soft curve and place the dorsal petal over a more definite curve. Allow them to dry. The central vein should be arranged so that the indentation is uppermost while the petals are drying over the curves.

Dry all petals for at least 24 hours before assembling the flower. Dust the petals as desired. Starting with the tongue, arrange the two lateral petals on either side of the tongue, and slightly behind it. Bind into place with fine rose wire. Add the two lower petals behind the two lateral petals, curving away from the tongue. Add the dorsal petal last. All petal bases should be in a line with one another at the point of wiring. Cover the rose wire with tape so that the petals appear to emerge from the stem.

Bleeding heart

These flowers look good cascading down the side of a cake. Fasten one large white stamen, preferably one with ridges, to the end of a 28-guage wire. Take a small piece of paste and fasten it directly over the stamen. Gently pinch the paste to make a fine oval rim around the stamen. Down the centre of the stamen, pinch out two fine wings at a 90° angle to the outer rim. Trim the ridge so that it is even. Gently pinch the paste on the wire to create a narrow neck. Fasten this firmly to the wire.

Choose a heart-shaped cutter smaller than the size of the final flower. Roll out a piece of paste so that it is dome shaped, and cut out a heart shape. Moisten the neck of the stamen/wing and insert the wire through the point of the heart shape cut from the dome. The wire should protrude through the central depression in the upper edge of the heart. Gently pinch the lower edges of the heart so that the petal narrow at the point. The upper curved edges of the heart should be a little

thicker than the petal at the point of the heart, but should be narrower than the centre of the petal.

Tint the central paste-covered stamen with yellow and green petal dust. Using a piece of pink paste, roll out and cut two heart shapes slightly larger than the heart cut for the central petal. Using a modelling knife, cut each heart in half, moisten the halves with a little egg white and fasten over one side of the central heart-shaped petal. Make sure that the join is not noticeable.

Take a tiny piece of pink paste, roll it into a ball, make a tiny baton and fasten this to the tip of the pink cut heart with a little egg white. Using a cocktail stick gently curve the baton outwards and upwards. The narrow end of the baton is fastened to the tip of the heart-shaped petal. Repeat for the other side. Curve the wire into a graceful arc.

Make a smaller flower in the same way, leaving less of the central heart-shaped petal protruding. The third shape, which is really just a pink heart with the paste-covered stamen protruding, forms a bud.

Filler Flowers

Small filler flowers are extremely important in a spray. It is no good having delicate, beautiful roses if they are displayed with clumsy, heavy filler flowers.

There are several ways of making filler flowers. The first is with cutters, which come with or without plungers.

You will need a collection of cutters, such as small blossom cutters, daisy cutters, small calyx and daphne cutters. Other necessary items include fine stamens with stiff stems, a selection of ball tools, including glass-headed pins inserted into dowelling, and a dense pad of foam rubber dusted with cornflour.

Small cutter flowers

Roll out a small piece of paste until it is translucent. Using a small blossom cutter with a plunger, cut a flower, drag the cutter gently along the surface of the board and eject the blossom onto the piece of foam rubber by depressing the plunger. Cut about 15 or 20 blossoms at a time. With a glass-headed pin, gently make a small hole in the centre of each blossom. Insert the thread of a stamen into the hole and pull into place. Just before it settles, pipe a tiny spot of royal icing into the centre of the flower. Pull the stamen into place and leave to dry.

The spot of royal icing must be very tiny, as a large spot will spread around the stamen and look unattractive. Another method is to pipe a spot of pale green royal icing behind the flower, at the point where the stamen and the flower meet. This will fasten them together and will look as though a calyx is attached to the flower.

Use a small blossom cutter without a plunger in the same way. Eject the blossom from the cutter by using a glass-headed pin or the tip of a paintbrush. If you press firmly onto the foam rubber with either of these objects, the flower will cup just as it does when using a plunger cutter, although this method does take longer. Fasten the blossom to the stamen in the same way.

Small calyx and daphne cutters can also be used in the same way. For an interesting variation, once the central cupping is made, turn the blossom over and jab each petal from the back with a glass-headed pin, paintbrush or small ball tool. This will cup each petal in the opposite direction. Make small holes with a pin, insert the stamens and continue as before.

All these small flowers should be used by taping them in small clusters on fine wires, which are then wired into the sprays.

All sugar flower arrangements and sprays need buds. If making tiny cutter flowers, it is almost impossible to make flower paste buds small enough. The easiest way to create tiny buds in the correct proportion is to use teardrop-shaped white stamens. Brush the base of the stamen with a little green petal dust and touch the tip with colour to match the tint of the flower. Buds are usually slightly deeper in colour than the opened flowers. The stamens are then taped onto a fine wire in an interesting, decreasing bunch.

Blossoms

Take a small piece of white paste and make a golf tee. Roll out the paste from the centre. Put the cutter over the centre and cut out the blossom. Gently drag the blossom along the board, and then across the edge of your hand to remove any rough edges. Push the blossom out of the cutter with the end of a paintbrush. Moisten the end of a fine wire with egg white and insert the wire into the flower. Insert the unmoistened end of the wire first, from the centre of the flower, ensuring that the wire comes out of the point at the back. Embed the moistened end of the wire in the point. If wished, mark the centre of the flower with the ribbed tool, which creates an interesting effect when the flower is petal dusted, or insert the point of a skewer or an anger tool into the centre to make a slight trumpet.

For another variation, press the small ball tool into each petal, one at a time, using the pad of a finger coated in white fat as a mat. Add three stamens to each flower, one longer than the others. When the flowers are dry, petal dust them. A tiny calyx can be painted on.

Daphne

Take a small piece of white paste and make a golf tee. Roll out the paste from the centre until it is translucent. Place the daphne cutter over the centre and cut out the flower. Gently drag the flower along the board and then across the edge of your hand. Eject the flower using a paint brush. Insert a moistened wire from the front of the flower. Enlarge the hole created by the wire insertion until there is a trumpet shaped depression. The wire should not show.

Roll the paste on the wire between your forefingers until a slender tube is created. Remove any paste that is untidy, or if the tube gets too long. Using the pad of your finger as a mat, gently indent each petal with a cocktail stick from the centre of the flower to the tip of the petal. Pinch the tip of each petal, bending the petals backwards at the same time. Two petals (opposite one another) should be arranged slightly behind the other two. By gently rolling the cocktail stick on these two rear petals they are also broadened slightly.

When the flower is dry, petal dust the back of the petals and the tube a rich pink. Add a brush of green to the base of the flower to act as a calyx. The upper surface of the petals should be left white. The petal dust will glow through the translucent petals.

Stephanotis

This flower is very often used in bridal bouquets. Take a small piece of very white paste and make a golf tee. Roll out the paste around the base until translucent. Place the small calyx cutter over the centre and cut out the flower. Loosen the base from the board and gently roll the tube between the little fingers until you have achieved a graceful curve to the back of the flower.

Open the throat of the flower with a skewer or anger tool. Insert a moistened wire into the centre. With the point of the dresden tool or the point of a paint brush gently indent each petal in the centre to a slight V-shape. Gently pinch the tips of each petal. Roll out a small piece of green paste. Using the tiny star cutter, cut a calyx. Thread it onto the wire, and moisten the base of the flower with a little egg white so that the calyx can be placed in position. Delicately shade the tube of the flower a creamy white.

Arum lily

Make a series of centres by attaching long, narrow pieces of paste to fine wire. The paste should protrude beyond the end of the wire, and should be rounded, not pointed at the tip. The centres should not have bulges at the sides, and should be one-half to two-thirds the depth of the petal. When the centre is dry, dip it into a little egg white and then into cornmeal.

These flowers come in waxy white, and a range of pinks and yellows. Roll out the paste until it is translucent. Cut the shape, cleaning it on the board and hand. Gently smooth the edge of the petal with a ball tool, but do not frill it. Moisten the straight edge at the base with a little egg white. Place the centre to the left of the petal. With a single flowing movement, roll the petal onto the centre using the thumb. Using a cocktail stick, gently roll back the petal, and pinch the tip between the finger and thumb, tugging it backwards gently at the same time. Dust the outside of the petal with colour, and brush on a little green where the flower joins the wire.

Daisy

First make the calyx. Make a golf tee of dark green paste. Cut out the calyx with the correct-sized cutter and insert a moistened wire through the centre. Make sure it is tightly attached. With the small ball tool, make an indentation in the centre of the calyx. Set aside to dry.

If using daisies in a spray, wire them in before adding the petals. Just the calyx gets wired in, or the petals may get knocked off. Leave enough space around each calyx for the petals.

Roll out the paste to a medium thickness. Cut out the petal, drag the cutter along the board, smooth off rough edges on the hand. Place the shape back on the board and with a cocktail stick press lines into each petal from the centre to the tip. Moisten the dry calyx with a little egg white. Place the petal on the calyx and, with the same ball tool used to shape the calyx, press the petals into place.

Take a very small piece of bright yellow paste. Press this into a piece of tulle until the centre has clear impressions left on it. Pick the centre up on the end of a pin and moisten the hollow with a little egg white. Place the centre into the hollow.

Primrose

Colour the paste a delicate lemony-yellow. Take a small ball of paste and make a golf tee. Roll out the paste until translucent. Place the cutter over the centre if using a metal cutter, or drop the centre into the hole if using a plastic cutter, and cut out the shape. Loosen the flower from the board and roll the tube between your fingers until slender.

Take a tiny piece of green paste, roll into a small ball, flatten it between your finger and the board. Attach it to the centre of the flower with a bit of egg white. Open the throat of the flower gently with a sati stick, making sure you penetrate the centre of the green spot. Gently swivel the stick to make a small centre. Insert a moistened wire through the centre. Insert one small green stamen so it appears just above the surface of the petal.

Soften the edge of each petal by rolling a cocktail stick around it, pressing against the pad of your finger. Use a little white fat on your finger so that the petals don't stick and break off. Don't frill the edge:

Finger Flowers

These flowers are not made with cutters. The basic shape is made by cutting the paste with a modelling knife, or by slightly hollowing a teardrop of paste and then cutting the petals with a pair of fine-bladed scissors. The flower is then enhanced by skilled use of fingers, cocktail sticks, etc. Because they are quick flowers, a calyx is not needed. Instead, the impression of a calyx is created by colouring.

Bouvardia

This attractive flower grows in clusters, but can be used most effectively in sprays and arrangements. Take a small piece of paste. Roll it into a ball, and then into a teardrop. Dip a skewer into cornflour, give it a sharp tap on the container and insert it into the broad base of the teardrop. The skewer should not be pushed into the teardrop for more than 5mm (¼in). Make four equal cuts around the circumference of the base of the teardrop. Remove from the skewer. Twirl the cut teardrop as you are putting the skewer down. This

helps to spread the petals slightly.

Take each petal between your thumb and forefinger, one at a time. Pinch the petals sharply. This makes a sharp V-shape. Hold the petals between forefinger and thumb and firmly tweak each one.

Moisten the end of a fine wire with egg white and pull it into the centre of the flower. Bury the wire in the base of the flower. Gently pinch the tip of each petal and open the throat if that is required. When the flower is dry, dust with colour, adding a little green dust where the base meets the wire to indicate a calyx.

soften it and broaden the petals slightly. Using the dresden tool, gently make a slight depression in the centre of each petal.

Arrange the petals. Petal dust the distinctive yellow markings in the centre of the flower. To make the calyx, take a piece of green paste. Press a cocktail stick onto it many times so it looks rather like corduroy. Paint a little egg white onto the base of the tube and arrange the green paste around the tube, joining it gently.

Make a mould from a real primrose leaf and use this for creating realistic leaves. Create the backward curl of the leaf by running a ball tool around the leaf just inside the outer edge.

Quick blossom

This is not a specific flower, just any five-petalled flower which is not named. Make as for Bouvardia up to the point when the wire is inserted, cutting five petals instead of four. This will give a flower with straight-edged petals. When the flower is dry, emphasis the centre with saffron yellow petal dust, with a tiny touch of green in the very centre. Petal dust the petals as required.

If you wish to alter the blossom slightly, proceed to the point where the petals have been cut. Pinch each petal firmly between your finger and thumb so that they become narrow. Tweak them to make pretty oval petals, and petal dust yellow in the centre with green for the calyx. A further alteration can be made by adding a few stamens.

Orange blossom

Take a small ball of very white paste. Roll it into a small cigar.

With a knitting needle roll this flat. Cut into a rectangle and then make short, sharp cuts along one long edge so that it looks like a comb.

Take six bright yellow, tiny stamens and a piece of 28-gauge wire. Hold the stamens and a piece of wire of the same length as the stamens in your left hand. With your right hand, firmly bind the long end of wire three times around the stamens. Bind the wire that is the same length as the stamens back down the long wire. The centre should be firm. The length of the stamens determines how large the flower will be. If the stamens are very long, the flower will be large. Trim any loose wire from the stamen knot. Moisten it with a little egg white and bind the fringed rectangle of paste to the knot, so that it surrounds the stamens. The stamens should protrude beyond the fringing. Set aside to dry.

Take a small ball of paste, make a teardrop and cut five equal petals on a skewer. Pinch each petal very firmly – the petals of an orange blossom are rather long, slender and curved. Tweak the petals, and then firmly pinch the tip of the petal giving it a graceful curve. Tip the fringing with a little orangy-yellow petal dust, and emphasise the colour of the stamens if necessary. Brush on a little green petal dust for the calyx.

Frilly flower

This is not an actual flower, but it is most attractive in a spray. Take a small ball of paste. Make a teardrop, insert a skewer and cut five equal petals. Tweak each petal, so that they are slightly square. Put a little white fat on the forefinger of your left hand. Place the first petal on the pad of your finger, and, with the point of a cocktail stick in the centre of the flower, roll the cocktail stick around the outer edge of the petal, keeping the pressure on the edge of the petal. It will spread and frill at the same time. Go right around the corner of the petal. Now curve the petal towards you. Continue until all the petals have been done. Emphasise the centre of the flower with the skewer and insert a moistened fine wire. Secure the flower to the wire and then put in a few stamens. When the flower is dry, petal dust very delicately.

Violet

Make a small ball of paste and place it on a skewer. Cut five petals, with one petal about one-third of the circumference of the teardrop base. Divide the remaining paste into four equal petals.

Another method is to cut a petal the width of the skewer. Turn the skewer and cut the remaining piece in half, and then halve each half. Twirl the flower. Leave the large petal and the petals on either side of it unpinched, but firmly pinch the two petals opposite the large one.

To make the lower three petals curve inwards, place the finger inside the flower and tweak. Place the finger outside the flower while tweaking the two long back petals. Pinch the tips of these two petals and make sure they curve backwards.

Moisten a fine wire and insert it into the flower. Cut one short, bright orangy-yellow stamen and nestle it into the centre of the flower. Allow the flower to dry and then decorate it. Paint delicate, veined lines on the three lower petals with a very fine brush. Mix a little cornflower blue petal dust into the violet colour and brush this on the outside petals only. Accentuate the edge of the petals with a little soft colour. Paint a tiny pointed calyx with paste colour. When the flower is completed, drop the head forward to prevent it from looking rigid.

To give a softer look to the

128

violet, after tweaking, frill the large petal gently with a cocktail stick on the pad of the finger, then gently bend it back.

To make violet buds, make a teardrop of paste and insert a wire into the broad base. Pinch the tip, and then pinch a point on the base. Petal dust the bud and paint on a calyx. Make glossy, dark green, heart-shaped leaves with veins fanning from the centre.

Pansy

Take a medium-sized ball of paste. Make a teardrop. Cut as for the violet. Tweak each petal as usual to make five square petals, one larger than the others.

Start working on the back petals. Place the cocktail stick point in the centre of the flower. Roll on the pad of the finger, as for the frilly flower. Curve the first petal out of the way when doing the second one. Repeat for the two side petals. Before frilling the final one, arrange the first four.

Moisten a fine wire with egg white, insert and fasten the flower firmly. Arrange the flower in the correct position, with the head slightly forward. Use the dresden tool or the back of a paint brush to lift the large petal by applying pressure to the centre. Allow the flower to dry.

Paint in the declicate, black veins on the three lower petals. Tint with violet back petals, soft yellow lower petals with brushings of violet, and tip all the petals with cornflower blue.

Quick rose

This is a very pretty flower, and quicker to make than the rose on page 104. Use delicately coloured paste as a base and then petal dust when the flower is dry.

The size of the flower is determined by the size of the piece of paste for the centre. All the small balls for the outer petals should be the same size. Make a hook with 26-gauge wire. Roll the first piece of paste into a cigar, but don't taper the ends too much. Gently roll out the cigar with a knitting needle. Finger out one side of the rectangle, making sure that the opposite edge remains plump and rounded to form the rounded base of the flower.

Paint a little egg white along the plump edge. Lift the petal onto the finger of the left hand. Place the hooked wire on the plump base.

Fasten a little paste over the hook with your thumb and then roll up the cigar. Make sure that the centre of the spiral is lower than the outer spirals. Don't fasten down the last part of the petal also.

Take a ball of paste for the next petal, and roll into a teardrop. Place it in the palm of your hand and flatten it with the forefinger of the other hand. Pinch out until the edge is very fine. Place a little egg white on the pointed base and insert this into the opening of the first spiralled petal. Now curve down the remainder of the spiralled petal, and curve back the petal edge as well; curve back the second petal.

Continue to add petals to the flower, overlapping the join of each previous petal until the rose is the size required. Neaten the lower edge, creating a hip with a cocktail stick. Allow to dry and then petal dust as required. Warmth is added to the flower if a little saffron yellow is touched into the centre of the rose and at the base of the petals where they are joined together. Paint a calyx onto the flower with paste colour, bringing the green up the petals at the joints, and covering the hip completely.

Quick rosebud: make a teardrop. Insert a moistened piece of 28-gauge wire through the broad base. Run a cocktail stick around the teardrop about one-quarter of the way from the base until a neat waistline has been created. Take a sharp knife and slash the upper portion of the bud from the waist to the tip in five places. Slide the knife into two slits and lift and twist gently to loosen the cut pieces. Gently pinch between your finger and thumb until a delicate rim is formed. Make sure that the tip remains pointed. If it has been distorted, work between fingers to make a point. Allow to dry. When the buds are dry, brush gently with the colour of the rose. Touch a little yellow under the lifted rims. Paint on a green calyx, taking the green mainly up the slashes. The sepals fit over the joins between the petals.

Lily-of-the-valley

Take a piece of fine wire, make a hook and cover with a small knob of paste. Take a medium-sized ball of paste, turn it into a teardrop and insert a small skewer. Cut six petals, and cut out a triangle between each petal. Pinch each petal, tugging backwards at the

same time. Tweak each tiny petal. Cut off some excess at the back of the flower, leaving a thick pad.

Insert a glass-headed pin stuck into a dowel into the centre of the flower. Use the ball of your thumb to smooth the cut-off base. When you have achieved the correct shape, carefully turn the tips of the petals back and outward.

Moisten the knob of paste on the fine wire and pull into place. Gently bend the wire into the required shape. Fasten the stamen in place with a little royal icing. Wire the flowers onto a fine wire, including a few round buds.

Hyacinth

Take a small piece of paste. Make a teardrop and insert a skewer. Cut six petals. Twirl the flower and then pinch each petal very hard. Tweak each petal and use a cocktail stick and the pad of your finger to make an indentation from the tip of each petal to the centre of the flower. Pinch the tip of each petal again. Insert a glass-headed pin into the centre of the flower, to create a slightly rounded base. Remove the pin, insert a hooked, moistened wire and set aside to dry. Tint the flower as desired.

Primula

Take a small ball of paste, make a teardrop and insert a skewer into the broad base. Cut five equal, fairly long petals. Now cut each petal in half, half the depth of the original cut. Make sure each cut is deep and clean. Remove the skewer, twirl the flower. Each petal should be clearly cut with a division in the centre.

Take the first petal between your finger and thumb. Spread the centre cut so a good V-shape is formed. Grasp the petal firmly and tweak strongly. If you have spread the petal sufficiently and tweaked hard enough you will now have a heart-shaped petal. Repeat this on the remaining petals. Re-insert the skewer to make a neat flower. Insert a moistened fine wire into the flower and set aside to dry. Tint the flower, accentuating the edge. Brush the centre with saffron yellow and a touch of green in the throat.

131

Flower Sprays

The basic principles for making sugar flower sprays are similar to those used by florists, but there are a few special factors to be considered. Sugar flowers are not as flexible as real flowers; crowd sugar flowers together and petals will break. Colours which look right in nature can look artificial when reproduced in sugar: understatement of colour is far better. Remember to keep the flowers in proportion with the cake.

Plan the spray when you design the cake. Make a sketch of the spray to the correct finished size. The most important things to bear in mind are colour, shape and proportion. Some ideas are more difficult to execute than others. Plan a simple design and execute it beautifully.

The approximate size of a spray should be about two-thirds the length of the cake top. The length of the spray should be one and a half times its width at the widest point. A spray is measured from the focal point, so if producing a straight spray, the focal point should be one-third of the way along from the rear and two-thirds from the tip.

The smallest, palest flowers must be at the extremities of the spray, and the heaviest, darkest flowers should be at, or near, the focal point. Dark colouring at the outer edge of a spray creates the impression of unbalanced heaviness. Allow enough room for each flower to breathe — to have enough surrounding space. Naturally, the spray should not look sparse, so if there seems to be a gap, add a flower even if it breaks the planned numerical order.

The most common spray shapes used in cake decoration are the vase containing an arrangement of flowers, oval, straight spray (waterfall spray), T-crescent, full crescent, posy and Hogarth curve. When selecting a spray for a cake, consider the overall impression. If a cake is upright, top it with a small vase containing flowers. Other wedding or tiered cakes look best when topped with a Hogarth curve, with the lower arm coming off the side of the cake. A T-crescent or a full crescent can look good on a single-tiered cake. Posies can be too bulky for anything but a very large cake.

As always in cake decorating, work as hygienically as possible. If you want the sprays to be attached to the cake, protect the cake from contamination which may be caused by wiring or binding. Use flower picks which have been made specifically to be inserted into a cake, or if not obtainable a good quality food-grade plastic barrier can be used.

Before starting a spray, assemble all the items necessary: sugar flowers and leaves; petal dust; paste colouring; brushes; water; tissues; 28-gauge wire; binding wire; stemtex; stripper; craft scissors; ribbon scissors; ribbons; and a large, thick pad of foam rubber to work over. Tint flowers to go with the cake: separate them into the various types and sizes; have the sketch showing the finished size of the spray. Remember that the flowers and foliage should blend together harmoniously.

Use green tape, cut into four, to bind the flowers to the main wires. Allow enough room between each flower so you can move them, and leave about 5mm (¼in) unbound below each flower. Don't have too many wires showing: hide them, where possible, with ribbon or foliage. Do not allow the separate pieces of a spray to end up with thick stems. Keep one wire going as the central wire, and cut off any excess from other wires before the bulk builds up. Make sure the flowers are securely in place before you cut off the excess. Keep any wires that are a reasonable length so that you can use them in another spray.

Remember that a spray is three-dimensional: it must look good from all angles. Look at the spray from every angle to ensure a good effect. The odd piece may be added once the spray is in place on the cake, but remember that loose pieces may come off during the delivery and smash other delicate work.

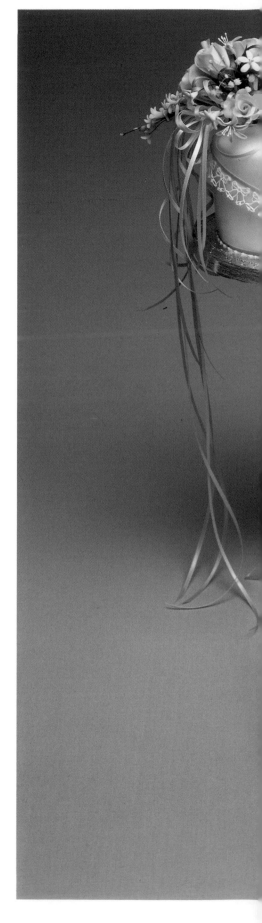

Ribbon Bows for Sprays

Swallow tail

This is used at the tip of the spray. Take a small piece of ribbon and fold it in half. Take a piece of 28-gauge wire, hold it so that one end is in line with the points of the ribbon, bind the long piece of wire tightly around the fold three times, then bend the short piece of wire back down and twist sharply so that the two wires are tightly bound together. Carefully trim the points of the ribbon.

Bounce bows

These are mainly used for filling gaps, instead of a flower or a leaf. Take a piece of ribbon, make a loop so that a thumb will fit in the gap and bring the end up alongside the ribbon, bind the long wire around the folded end of the ribbon, bend the short wire back down, twist sharply, cut off any excess wire, trim the point neatly.

Double bounce bows, no tail

Make two loops next to one another, as for the single bounce bow. The loops should look heart-shaped from the side. Bind the wire around the folded ends as before, and cut off excess ribbon as close to the wire as possible.

Double bounce bows with longer trailers

Make two loops next to one another. Fold the ribbon alongside the loops to make the trailers. Twist the ribbon once and bring it back to the base. Cut off the excess ribbon, and bind the wire on as before. Cut the ribbon at the twist and trim to a point. These bows are used to decorate the base of a spray, and the trailers are arranged along the surface of the cake. Run the blade of a pair of scissors or a knife sharply along the underside of the ribbon to make it curve attactively.

Figure-of-eight bow

Take piece of ribbon in your right hand and bring the end around so that when you lay it on the piece you started with it lies flat. Continue the curve in the other direction, and repeat so that the ribbon comes in from one direction and goes out in the other direction. Place a piece of 28-gauge wire under the ribbon and fold the ribbon around it on both sides. Hold the ribbon and twist the ends of the wire together firmly. Figure-of-eight bows are usually used in twos, threes or fours. Cross one bow over the other at right angles with the wires together. Bind in place with binding wire or cut tape. Trim off all but one wire.

Crescent

This is a most attractive shape to use on a round or petal-shaped cake. Make two identical sprays of flowers and a single, slender, shorter one. Bend the main wires down at a 90° angle so that the broad ends of each spray point at one another. Add the shorter spray at the junction of the first two sprays, pointing away from them (the broader end of this spray joins the others). Cover the join with two or three bunches of figure-of-eight bows and then pull in the focal point on top. Add single flowers and additional slender sprays where necessary. Bind all the ends together and cut them off neatly.

Vase of flowers

Choose a pretty, small vase with a heavy base to prevent it from overbalancing while being filled. Fasten the vase securely into a flat-based container to further ensure that it will not fall over. Make sure the vase is clean and polished. Fill the vase with green sugarpaste.

Decide on the shape of the arrangement. If using hanging flowers like fuchsias, remember to counterbalance the downward curve with a lifted section. Use the double bounce bow with trailers interspaced between fuchsias. Ribbons trailing from the vase to the surface of the cake are attractive.

Hogarth curve

This can be very attractive on the top of a wedding cake. Make two sprays, one longer than the other. The shorter one should be taped in the round so it is symmetrical from all angles. The longer, broader spray rests on the cake so there should be no flowers on the underside. Add two or three figure-of-eight bows, and as many small sprays as necessary. Pull in the focal point. Position the spray so that it curves over the edge. Fill in any gaps with flowers, adding another large flower towards the back.

Oval

Make four sprays of flowers, one longer than the others to make the central column. Bind together to form a cross. Pull in the focal point at the centre of the cross. Gradually add slender sprays of small flowers and ribbons to fill out the oval effect.

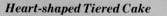

Heart-shaped Tiered Cake
The long ribbons of this Hogarth curve make an elegant finishing touch to this tiered wedding cake. The sugarpasted hearts measure 20cm (8in) and 15cm (6in), and the heart-shaped boards are positioned on a perspex stand. The co-ordinating oval spray looks perfect when placed next to the simply decorated cake.

T-Crescent

Make one large spray, and another the same width, but half the length. Make a number of small, slender flower sprays. Have several figure-of-eight bows ready. Join the sprays as for the waterfall, filling the join with the bows. Add a few slender flower sprays. Position the focal point, remembering to keep the profile correct. Add separate shorter sprays and individual flowers where needed.

Posy

This is a completely round, formal arrangement of flowers. A Victorian posy has a rose as the focal point. Posies are usually finished off with frills.

Make six identical small sprays and six sprays of foliage, all the length of the radius of the finished posy. Make four figure-of-eight bows and join them together. Fasten the six small sprays to resemble the spokes of a wheel. Fill any gaps with individual flowers and pull in the focal point. From the side, the spray must be hemispherical. Fit posy into a frill.

Straight spray (waterfall)

Make four sprays of flowers, three of them the same length, which should be half the length of the longer one. The longer spray should also be broader than the others.

Bind the sprays together to make a cross. Look at the spray from the side to visualize a dome for positioning the height of the focal point. Once you have assessed the height, add two or three figure-of-eight bows on top of the join where the four sprays cross. Pull in the focal point and gradually add slender sprays of small flowers and larger flowers until an attractive balance has been achieved.

Pastillage

Pastillage can be made in many different ways. One form of pastillage is flower paste, which can be used for making cards, or moulding slippers, bells and other objects. Most attractive painted cards can be produced, and cards can be constructed so that an arrangement of flowers protrudes through them.

Cards

Very simple cards can be made by rolling out flower paste until it is translucent and then cutting out the appropriate shape, folding it in half and allowing it to dry in that position, supported by a piece of cardboard bent to the correct shape. Additional decoration such as frilled edges or cut-outs should be done before the card is set to dry. Simple decorations such as appliquéd flowers or embroidered motifs are most suitable for this style of card.

More complicated sugar cards, including three-dimensional ones, which stand upright, can also be made. Roll out the paste as thinly as possible. If decorating the card with a cut-out piece, remove while the paste is still pliable. Trim the edges and make holes if joining the pieces together with ribbon. The cut pieces should be put on a lightly cornfloured, completely flat surface to dry. Turn the pieces repeatedly so they do not buckle.

Slipper

There are now many attractive slipper moulds on the market. Roll out the paste until it is about 5mm (¼in) thick. Lightly dust the smooth side of the paste with cornflour. Push the paste into the mould and work until it is extremely fine, ensuring that the edges are very straight and don't have any nicks. Each nick will mean a gap when you join the two sides of the slipper together. Keep taking the paste out of the mould to prevent it sticking. If it seems to be catching, dust a little more cornflour onto the outside of the slipper and press it back in the mould.

Leave the moulded paste to dry for about 48 hours. When set, make the other side of the slipper in the same way. Remember not to produce two of the same side unless you want to produce a pair of shoes.

Once you are sure you have a clean, neat finish, dampen the edge of the unset slipper in the mould with egg white. Press the dried half on top of the damp one and help them to join evenly. Leave to dry for another 48 hours before removing from the mould.

Remove the slipper from the mould. Gently rub any rough edges down with an emery board or fine sandpaper, and finish it off.

Roll out a piece of paste, moisten

it with egg white, place the slipper on it and cut out a sole and heel. This hides the bottom joins. Don't bother to hide the join at the back, as most shoes have them. The join down the heel can be disguised by working in some softened flower paste which can be rubbed down when dry. A little royal icing can also be worked in. The join at the front of the slipper is best disguised by making it look as though it has an embroidered or jewelled buckle attached. Small hearts are very

attractive for wedding cakes.

For a different look, embroider a floral design or use cornelli work over the slipper to look like a brocade shoe. This is done after filling in the crack with a little softened flower paste, allowing it to dry and sanding it down.

Another method of finishing is to fill in the cracks with a little royal icing, smoothed down with a damp brush. Set aside to dry, then dip the whole slipper into royal icing of a run-out consistency. Place on cling

film or silicone paper to dry. Gently sand off any excess icing that may have collected at the base of the shoe. If the first coating isn't perfect, dip it again and allow to dry again before sanding off the excess. Lustre colour gives a lovely, satiny finish to the slipper.

Pastillage slippers are very pretty ornaments for wedding cakes, either on their own, surrounded by moulded flowers, or with a cascading arrangement of sugar flowers and ribbons.

PRINTED IN BELGIUM BY
proost
INTERNATIONAL BOOK PRODUCTION